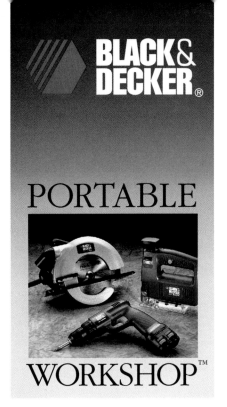

BLACK & DECKER®

PORTABLE

WORKSHOP™

Basic Wood Projects
with Portable Power Tools

Yard & Garden Furnishings

D0579448

Copyright © 1996 Cy DeCosse Incorporated
5900 Green Oak Drive, Minnetonka, Minnesota 55343
1-800-328-3895 All rights reserved
Printed in U.S.A.

Credits

Group Executive Editor: Paul Currie
Project Director: Mark Johanson
Associate Creative Director: Tim Himsel
Managing Editor: Kristen Olson
Project Manager: Lori Holmberg
Lead Project Designer: Jim Huntley
Editors: Mark Biscan, Steve Meyer
Editor & Technical Artist: Jon Simpson
Editorial Assistant: Andrew Sweet
Lead Art Director: Gina Seeling
Technical Production Editor: Greg Pluth
Project Designer: Steve Meyer
Contributing Draftsman: John T. Drigot

*Vice President of Photography
 & Production:* Jim Bindas
Copy Editor: Janice Cauley
Shop Supervisor: Phil Juntti
Lead Builder: John Nadeau
Builders: Troy Johnson, Rob Johnstone
Production Staff: Laura Hokkanen, Tom
 Hoops, Jeanette Moss, Christopher Ostrom,
 Gary Sandin, Mike Schauer, Mike Sipe,
 Brent Thomas, Kay Wethern

Creative Photo Coordinator:
 Cathleen Shannon
Studio Manager: Marcia Chambers
Lead Photographer: Rebecca Schmitt
Photography Assistant: Greg Wallace
Production Manager: Stasia Dorn
Printed on American paper by:
 Inland Press 99 98 97 96 / 5 4 3 2 1

CY DeCOSSE INCORPORATED

Chairman/CEO: Philip L. Penny
Chairman Emeritus: Cy DeCosse
President/COO: Nino Tarantino
Executive V.P./Editor-in-Chief:
 William B. Jones

Created by: The editors of Cy DeCosse
 Incorporated, in cooperation with Black
 & Decker. ● BLACK&DECKER is a trademark
 of the Black & Decker Corporation and
 is used under license.

Library of Congress
Cataloging-in-Publication Data

Yard and garden furnishings.
        p. cm.—(Portable workshop)
   At head of title: Black & Decker.
   ISBN   0-86573-668-5 (hardcover).

1. Outdoor furniture. 2. Woodwork. 3. Garden orna-
ments and furniture—Design and construction.
I. Cy DeCosse Incorporated.
II. Black & Decker Corporation (Towson, MD)
III. Series.
TT197.5.09Y37   1996
684.1' 8—dc20   96-24422

Contents

Introduction 4

Tools & Materials 5

Projects

Picnic Table For Two 8

Park Bench 12

Firewood Shelter 18

Trellis Planter. 22

Driveway Marker 26

Sundial 30

Yard & Garden Cart. 34

Backyard Fire Pit 40

Fire Pit Bench. 44

Trash Can Corral 48

Luminary. 52

Garden Bridge 56

Fold-up Lawn Seat 62

Gardener's Tote. 66

Plant Boxes. 70

Compost Bin. 74

Birdfeeder Stand 78

Tree Surround 82

Prairie Windmill. 88

Doghouse 92

Introduction

Even the most meticulously landscaped yard or garden will benefit from original, practical furnishings. With the right combination of form and function, even simple items like picnic tables and yard benches can raise the standards of your outdoor spaces. Whether you enjoy simple relaxation time in the backyard or down-and-dirty work in the garden, you need inexpensive, yet visually pleasing, furnishings to get the most out of your valuable time. With a quick glance through *Yard & Garden Furnishings* you'll see stylish little items like a decorative luminary and a working sundial, as well as steady workhorses like a yard-and-garden cart and a firewood shelter. The projects contained in this book make life a little easier for anyone who enjoys the outdoors. Best of all, they are designed for simplicity—you don't need to be an accomplished woodworker to build them.

Yard & Garden Furnishings is a book of plans offering you detailed information in the form of step-by-step instructions, full-color photographs, complete cutting and shopping lists and precise construction drawings for each of the 20 yard and garden furnishings. From a striking, decorative garden bridge to a contemporary doghouse, you'll be guided through the projects every step of the way.

With the Black & Decker® *Portable Workshop*™ series, you don't need to be an expert with power tools to create useful, attractive projects. Every item in this book can be built with basic hand tools and portable power tools you probably already own. Although you don't need a lot of experience working with basic hand tools to get the job done, you may want to practice using them on scraps of wood before you start the actual projects.

The Black & Decker® *Portable Workshop*™ series gives weekend do-it-yourselfers the ability to build great home projects. Ask your local bookseller for information on other volumes in this innovative new series.

NOTICE TO READERS

This book provides useful instructions, but we cannot anticipate all of your working conditions or the characteristics of your materials and tools. For safety, you should use caution, care, and good judgment when following the procedures described in this book. Consider your own skill level and the instructions and safety precautions associated with the various tools and materials shown. Neither the publisher nor Black & Decker® can assume responsibility for any damage to property, injury to persons, or losses incurred as a result of misuse of the information provided.

Organizing Your Worksite

Portable power tools and hand tools offer a level of convenience that is a great advantage over stationary power tools. But using them safely and conveniently requires some basic housekeeping. Whether you are working in a garage, a basement, or outdoors, it is important that you establish a flat, dry holding area where you can store tools. Set aside a piece of plywood on sawhorses, or dedicate an area of your workbench for tool storage, and be sure to return tools to that area once you are finished with them. It is also important that all waste, including lumber scraps and sawdust, be disposed of in a timely fashion. Check with your local waste disposal department before throwing away any large scraps of building materials or any finishing-material containers.

> ### Safety Tips
> •*Always wear eye and hearing protection when operating power tools and performing any other dangerous activities.*
> •*Choose a well-ventilated work area when cutting or shaping wood and when using finishing products.*

Tools & Materials

At the start of each project, you will find a set of symbols that show which power tools are used to complete the project as it is shown (see below). You will also need a set of basic hand tools: a hammer, screwdrivers, tape measure, a level, a combination square, C-clamps, and pipe or bar clamps. You also will find a shopping list of all the construction materials you will need. Miscellaneous materials and hardware are listed with the cutting list that accompanies the construction drawing. When buying lumber, note that the "nominal" size of the lumber is usually larger than the "actual size." For example, a 2 × 4 is actually 1½ × 3½".

Power Tools You Will Use

Circular saw to make straight cuts. For long cuts and rip-cuts, use a straight-edge guide. Install a carbide-tipped combination blade for most projects.

Drills: use a cordless drill for drilling pilot holes and counterbores, and to drive screws; use an electric drill for sanding and grinding tasks.

Jig saw for making contoured cuts and internal cuts. Use a combination wood blade for most projects where you will cut pine, cedar or plywood.

Power sander to prepare wood for a finish and to smooth out sharp edges. Owning several power sanders (⅓-sheet, ¼-sheet, and belt) is helpful.

Belt sander for resurfacing rough wood. Can also be used as a stationary sander when mounted on its side on a flat worksurface.

Router to cut decorative edges and roundovers in wood. As you gain more experience, use routers for cutting grooves (like dadoes) to form joints.

Finishing Your Project

Sand all surfaces to remove rough spots and splinters, using medium-grit (120 to 150) sandpaper. Insert wood plugs into screw counterbores and sand until smooth. Fine finish-sanding is usually not necessary for unpainted exterior projects, but cover nail and screw heads with wood putty, then sand with 180-grit sandpaper if you are painting. Most projects in this book are finished with exterior wood stain or clear wood sealer. Look for products that block UV rays, and follow the manufacturer's directions for application. When painting, use exterior primer, then apply enamel or glossy exterior paint.

Picnic Table For Two

*Turn a quiet corner of your yard into an intimate setting for dining
alfresco with this compact picnic table.*

CONSTRUCTION MATERIALS

Quantity	Lumber
1	2 × 8" × 6' cedar
1	2 × 6" × 8' cedar
3	2 × 4" × 8' cedar
3	1 × 6" × 8' cedar
3	1 × 2" × 8' cedar

A picnic table doesn't
have to be a clumsy,
uncomfortable family
feeding trough. In this project,
we created a unique picnic
table that's just the right size for
two people to enjoy. Portable
and lightweight, it can be set
in a corner of your garden, beneath a shade tree or on your
deck or patio to enhance your
outdoor dining experiences.
The generously proportioned
tabletop can be set with full
table settings for a formal meal
in the garden, but it is intimate
enough for sharing a cool bev-
erage with a special person as
you watch the sun set. Made
with plain dimensional cedar,
this picnic table for two is
sturdy and long-lasting as well.

OVERALL SIZE:
28" HIGH
30¼" WIDE
62" LONG

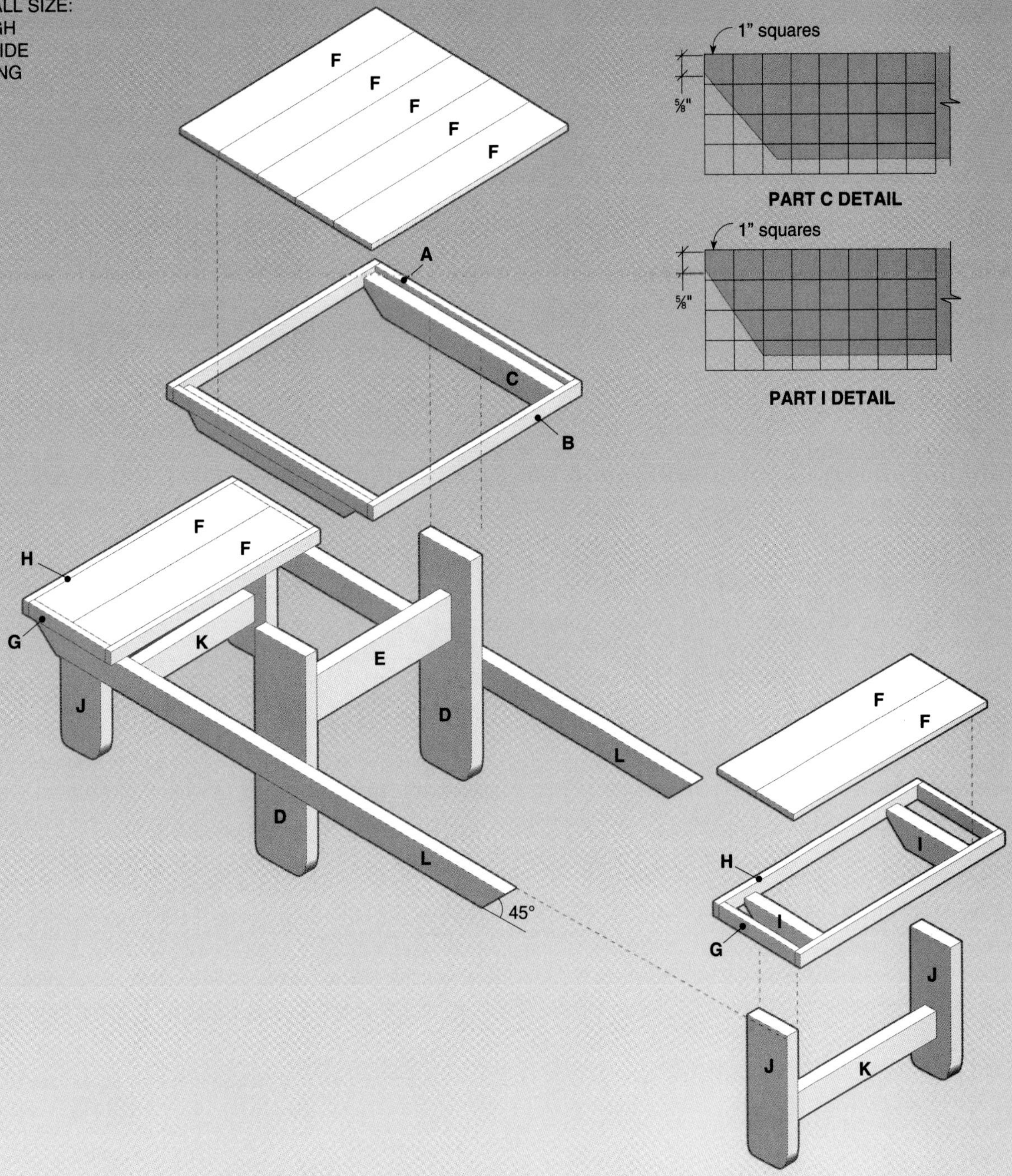

F
F
F
F
F
A
C
B
1" squares
⅝"
PART C DETAIL
1" squares
⅝"
PART I DETAIL
H
F
F
G
K
E
J
D
D
L
L
45°
F
F
H
I
I
G
J
J
K

Cutting List				
Key	**Part**	**Dimension**	**Pcs.**	**Material**
A	Tabletop frame	⅞ × 1½ × 27¾"	2	Cedar
B	Tabletop frame	⅞ × 1½ × 30"	2	Cedar
C	Table stringer	1½ × 3½ × 27¾"	2	Cedar
D	Table leg	1½ × 7¼ × 27¼"	2	Cedar
E	Table stretcher	1½ × 5½ × 22½"	1	Cedar
F	Slat	⅞ × 3½ × 28¼"	9	Cedar

Cutting List				
Key	**Part**	**Dimension**	**Pcs.**	**Material**
G	Bench frame	⅞ × 1½ × 11¼"	4	Cedar
H	Bench frame	⅞ × 1½ × 30"	4	Cedar
I	Bench stringer	1½ × 3½ × 11¼"	4	Cedar
J	Bench leg	1½ × 5½ × 15¼"	4	Cedar
K	Bench stretcher	1½ × 3½ × 22½"	2	Cedar
L	Cross rail	1½ × 3½ × 68"	2	Cedar

Materials: Moisture-resistant glue, brass or galvanized deck screws (1⅝", 2½"), finishing materials.

Note: Measurements reflect the actual size of dimensional lumber.

Make triangular cutoffs at the ends on the table stringers, using a circular saw.

Install the tabletop slats by driving screws through the tabletop frame and into the ends of the slats.

Directions:
Picnic Table For Two

BUILD THE TABLETOP. The tabletop for the picnic table is made from 1 × 6 cedar slats wrapped with a 1 × 2 frame. Start by cutting the tabletop frame pieces (A, B), the table stringers (C) and the table slats (F). Sand the parts, then mark triangular cutoffs at each end of the stringers by drawing cutting lines that start 2½" in from one end and connect with a point at the same end, ⅝" in from the opposite edge of the board (see Diagram, page 9). Miter-cut along the lines with a circular saw to make the cutoffs **(photo A).** Fasten the shorter tabletop frame pieces (A) to the sides of the stringers. The tops of the frame pieces should extend ⅞" above the tops of the stringers, and the ends should be flush. Use moisture-resistant glue and 1⅝" deck screws to attach the frame pieces to the stringers. Drive the screws through countersunk pilot holes. Then, position the longer tabletop frame pieces (B) so they overlay the ends of the shorter frame pieces, and fasten them together with glue and screws to complete the frames. Next, set the slats inside the frame so the ends of the slats rest on the stringers. Space them evenly, about ⅜" apart. Drive two screws through countersunk pilot holes in the tabletop frame, and into each end of each slat, starting with the two end slats **(photo B).**

MAKE & ATTACH THE TABLE-LEG ASSEMBLY. Two legs with rounded bottoms are attached to the centers of the stringers to support the tabletop. A single stretcher is attached between the legs for stability. Cut the table legs (D) and table stretcher (E). Use a compass to draw a roundover curve with a 1½" radius on the corners of one end of each leg. These ends will be the bottoms of the legs. Cut the curves with a jig saw. Press an end of the stretcher against the inside face of one of the table legs, 16" up from the bottom of the leg and centered side to side. Trace the outline of the stretcher onto the leg, and repeat the procedure on the other leg. Drill two evenly spaced pilot holes through the stretcher outlines on the legs, and countersink the holes on the outside faces of the legs. Attach the stretcher with glue and 2½" deck screws driven through the pilot holes and into the ends of the stretcher. To attach the table-leg assembly, turn the tabletop upside down, and apply glue to the table stringers where they will contact the legs. Position the legs in place within the tabletop frame, and attach them by driving 2½" deck screws through the legs and into the table stringers **(photo C).**

BUILD THE BENCH TOPS. The bench tops are very similar in design to the tabletop. Start by cutting the bench frame pieces (G, H) and bench stringers (I). Miter-cut the ends of the bench stringers in the same way you cut the table stringers, starting ⅝" down from the top edge and 2" in from the ends on the bottom edges. Assemble the frame pieces into two rectangular frames by driving screws through the longer frame

Position the table legs inside the tabletop frame, and attach them to the table stringers.

Set the bench legs against the outer faces of the stringers. Attach the stretcher between the legs, then attach the legs to the stringers.

pieces and into the ends of the shorter frame pieces. Turn the bench frames upside down, and center the bench slats inside them so the outer edges of the slats are flush against the frame. Attach the slats by driving 1⅝" deck screws through the frames and into the ends of the slats. Attach the stringers inside the frame so the tops of the stringers are flat against the undersides of the slats, 3" in from each frame end. Use glue and 1⅝" deck screws driven through the angled ends of the stringers and into the undersides of the slats. Be careful to locate the screws so they are far enough away from the ends of the stringers that they do not stick out through the tops of the slats after they are driven. The stringers are not attached directly to the bench frames.

BUILD THE BENCH LEGS. Start by cutting the bench legs (J) and bench stretchers (K). Use a compass to draw a roundover curve with a 1½" radius on the corners of one end of each leg. Cut the roundovers with a jig saw. Center the tops of the bench legs against the outside

faces of the bench stringers. Attach the bench legs to the bench stringers with glue and countersunk 2½" deck screws, driven through the stringers and into the legs. Position the bench stretchers against the inside faces of the bench legs, 3½" up from the bench leg bottoms. Glue the bench stretchers, and attach them between the legs with countersunk 2½" deck screws **(photo D).**

JOIN THE TABLE & BENCHES. Cut the cross rails (L) to length, miter-cutting the ends at a 45° angle (see *Diagram*). Position the benches so the ends of the cross rails are flush with the outside ends of the bench frames. Apply glue, and attach the cross rails to the bench legs with countersunk 2½" deck screws. Stand the benches up, and center the table legs between the cross rails. Apply glue to the joints between cross rails and legs, then clamp the table legs to the cross rails, making sure the parts are perpendicular **(photo E).** Secure the parts by driving several 2½" deck screws through the cross rails and into the outside face of each leg.

APPLY FINISHING TOUCHES. Sand all the sharp edges and flat surfaces of the picnic table, then apply a nontoxic wood sealant, like linseed oil, to protect the wood and keep it from turning gray.

Center the table within the cross rails, and clamp it in place.

Park Bench

This attention-grabbing park bench is a real showpiece that can transform even a plain yard into a formal garden.

CONSTRUCTION MATERIALS

Quantity	Lumber
5	2 × 4" × 8' pine
1	2 × 2" × 4' pine
4	1 × 6" × 8' pine

Add color and style to your backyard or garden with this bright, elegant park bench. Some careful jig saw work is all it takes to make the numerous curves and contours that give this bench a sophisticated look. But don't worry if your cuts aren't all perfect: the shapes are decorative, so the bench will still work just fine. In fact, if you prefer a simpler appearance, you can build the park bench with all straight parts, except the roundovers at the bottoms of the legs. But if you are willing to do the extra work, you're sure to be pleased with the final result—we certainly were, and that's why we finished it with bright red paint so no one would miss it.

OVERALL SIZE:
38" HIGH
23" DEEP
52" LONG

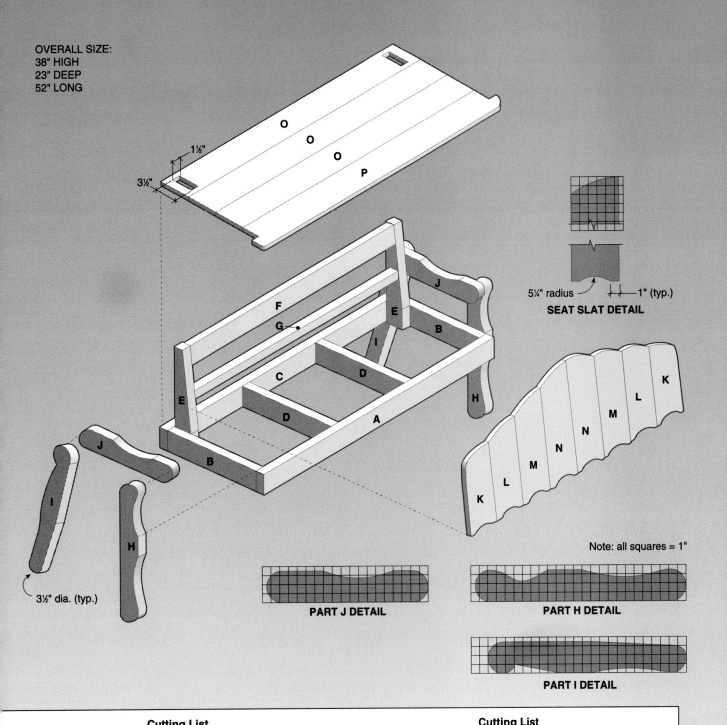

1½"

3½"

5¼" radius — 1" (typ.)

SEAT SLAT DETAIL

3½" dia. (typ.)

Note: all squares = 1"

PART J DETAIL

PART H DETAIL

PART I DETAIL

Key	Part	Dimension	Pcs.	Material
A	Front rail	1½ × 3½ × 49"	1	Pine
B	Side rail	1½ × 3½ × 20¼"	2	Pine
C	Back rail	1½ × 3½ × 46"	1	Pine
D	Cross rail	1½ × 3½ × 18¾"	2	Pine
E	Post	1½ × 3½ × 18"	2	Pine
F	Top rail	1½ × 3½ × 43"	1	Pine
G	Bottom rail	1½ × 1½ × 43"	1	Pine
H	Front leg	1½ × 3½ × 24½"	2	Pine

Cutting List

Key	Part	Dimension	Pcs.	Material
I	Rear leg	1½ × 3½ × 23"	2	Pine
J	Armrest	1½ × 3½ × 18½"	2	Pine
K	End slat	¾ × 5½ × 14"	2	Pine
L	Outside slat	¾ × 5½ × 16"	2	Pine
M	Inside slat	¾ × 5½ × 18"	2	Pine
N	Center slat	¾ × 5½ × 20"	2	Pine
O	Seat slat	¾ × 5½ × 49"	3	Pine
P	Seat nose slat	¾ × 5½ × 52"	1	Pine

Materials: Moisture-resistant glue, deck screws (1¼", 2½"), finishing materials.

Note: All measurements reflect the actual size of dimensional lumber.

Use a router or sander to round over the sharp bottom edges and corners of the completed seat frame.

Attach the seat slats and nose slat to the top of the seat frame with glue and deck screws.

Directions: Park Bench

BUILD THE SEAT FRAME. The seat frame is made by assembling rails and cross rails to form a rectangular unit. Start by cutting the front rail (A), side rails (B), back rail (C) and cross rails (D) to size. Sand all the parts with medium-grit sandpaper to smooth out any rough spots after cutting. Fasten the side rails to the front rail with moisture-resistant glue and 2½" deck screws, driven through the front rail and into the side rail ends. Counterbore the pilot holes to accept ⅜"-dia. wood plugs. Make sure the top and bottom edges of the side rails are flush with the top and bottom edges of the front rails. Attach the back rail between the side rails with glue and counterbored deck screws, driven through the side rails and into the ends of the back rail. Keep the back

rail flush with the ends of the side rails. Use glue and deck screws to fasten the two cross rails between the front and back rails, 14½" in from the inside face of each side rail. These cross rails provide structural support and help support the seat slats, which are attached to the top of the frame later in the assembly process. Complete the seat frame by rounding the bottom edges and corners with a router and a ⅜"-dia. roundover bit **(photo A)** or a hand sander.

MAKE THE SEAT SLATS. The very front seat slat, called the nose slat, has side cutouts to accept the front legs, and the back seat slat has cutouts, called mortises, to accept the posts that support the backrest.

Start by cutting the seat nose slat (P) and one seat slat (O) to size. To mark the 2 × 4 cutout at each end of the nose slat, use the end of a 2 × 4 as a template. Position the 2 × 4 on the seat slat at each end, 1½" in from the back edge and 1½" in from the end. The long sides of the 2 × 4 should be parallel to the ends of the back seat slat. Trace the outline of the 2 × 4 onto the slat. Drill a starter hole within the outline, and make the cutout with a jig saw. Then, use a jig saw to cut a 3"-long × 1½"-wide notch at each end of the nose slat, starting at the back edge (see *Diagram*, page 13). Sand the notches and mortises with a file or a thin sanding block.

ATTACH THE SEAT SLATS. The seat slats are attached to the top of the seat frame, parallel to the front and back rails. Cut the rest of the seat slats (O) to size, then lay the slats on the seat frame so the ends of the slats are flush with

---

TIP

Making smooth contour cuts with a jig saw can be a little tricky. To make it easier, install fairly thick saw blades, because they are less likely to "wander" with the grain of the wood. Using a scrolling jig saw will also help, since they are easier to turn than standard jig saws.

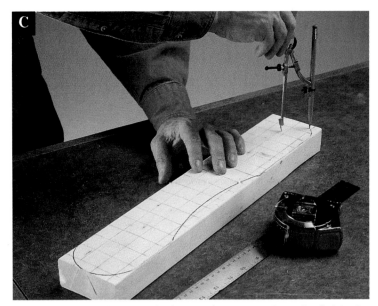

After drawing a 1" grid on the legs and armrests, draw the finished shape of the parts, following the Grid Patterns on page 13.

the frame, and the nose slat overhangs equally at the sides of the frame. Draw reference lines onto the tops of the seat slats and nose slat, directly over the top of each rail in the frame. These lines will be used to mark drilling points before attaching the slats to the seat frame. Mark two drilling points on each line on each slat, ¾" in from the front and from the back of the slat. Drill counterbored pilot holes at the drilling points. Sand the seat slats and nose slat, and attach them to the seat frame with glue and 1¼" deck screws **(photo B),** driven through the slats and into the frame and cross rails. Start with the front and back slats, and space the inner slats evenly.

MAKE THE LEGS & ARMRESTS. The front legs (H), rear legs (I) and armrests (J) are shaped using the *Grid Patterns* on page 13. First, cut workpieces for the parts to the full sizes shown in the *Cutting List*. Use a pencil to draw a 1"-square grid pattern on each workpiece. Then, use

the grid patterns as a reference for drawing the shapes onto the workpieces **(photo C)**—it will help if you enlarge the patterns on a photocopier or draw them to a larger scale on a piece of graph paper first. Cut out the shapes with a jig saw, then sand the contour cuts smooth. Use a drum sander mounted in your electric drill for best sanding results.

ATTACH THE LEGS. The front and rear legs are attached to the armrests, flush with the front and rear ends. Use glue and counterbored deck screws to fasten the front legs to the outside faces of the armrests, using a framing square to make sure the legs are perpendicular to the armrests.

Temporarily fasten the rear legs to the outside faces of the armrests with a centered, counterbored screw, driven through the rear leg and into the armrest. The rear leg must, for now, remain adjustable on the armrest. Once the rear legs have been positioned correctly against the seat, you will attach them permanently to the armrests. Clamp the seat to the legs. The front of the edge of the seat should be 16¾" up from the bottoms of the front legs. The back of the seat should be 14¼" up from the bottoms of the rear legs. Position square wood spacers between the seat and each armrest to keep the arm- rest parallel to the frame. Adjust the rear legs so their back edges are flush with the top corners of the side rails. The rear legs extend slightly beyond the back of the seat frame. Drive counterbored deck screws through the front and rear legs and into the side rails, then drive an additional screw through each rear leg into the

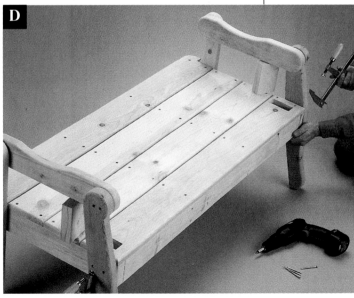

Carefully clamp the leg frames to the seat, and attach them with glue and counterbored screws.

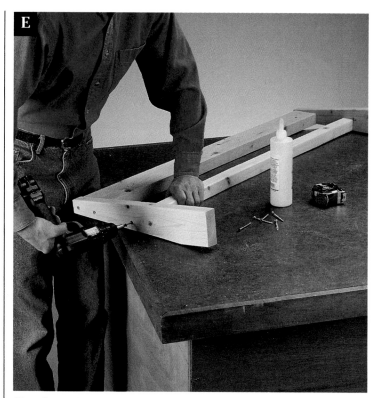

Glue the ends of the top and bottom rails, then drive deck screws through the posts to attach them to the rails.

armrests to permanently secure the rear legs in position. Unclamp the leg assemblies, and remove them from the frame **(photo D).** Apply glue to the leg assemblies where they join the frame, and reattach the legs and armrests using the same screw holes.

BUILD THE BACK FRAME. The back frame is made by attaching a top rail (F) and bottom rail (G) between two posts (E). Once the back frame has been built, it is inserted into the mor-

tises in the rear seat slats to form a backrest. Before you attach the rails, cut tapers on the front edges of the posts. The tapered posts will create a backward slope so the back slats make a more comfortable backrest when they are attached. When you attach the rails between the posts, make sure they are flush with the front edges of the posts. Cut the posts, top rail and bottom rail to size. Mark a tapered cutting line on each post, starting 1½" in from the back edge, at the top. Extend the line so it meets the front edge 3½" up from the bottom. Cut the taper in each post, using a circular saw or jig saw. Use glue and deck screws to fasten the top rail between the posts so the front face of the top rail is flush with the front (tapered) edge of each post. The tops of the posts and top rail should also be flush. Posi-

tion the bottom rail between the posts so its bottom edge is 9" up from the bottoms of the posts. Make sure the front face of the bottom rail is flush with the front edges of the posts. Attach the parts with glue and counterbored 2½" deck screws **(photo E).** Use a router with a ⅜"-dia. roundover bit, or a hand sander, to round over the back edges of the back frame.

MAKE THE BACK SLATS. The back slats are shaped on their tops and bottoms to create a scalloped effect when they are attached. Keep in mind, if you'd rather not spend the time cutting these contours, you can simply cut the slats to length and round over the top edges. Start by cutting the end slats (K), outside slats (L), inside slats (M) and center slats (N) to length. Draw a 1"-square grid pattern on one slat, then draw the shape shown in the *Slat Detail* on page 13 onto the slat. Then, mark a 5¼"-radius scalloped cutout at the bottom of the slat, using a compass. Cut the slat to shape with a jig saw, and sand smooth any rough spots or saw marks. Use the completed slat as a template to trace the same profile on the tops and bottoms of the remaining slats **(photo F),** and cut them to shape with a jig saw. Sand the cuts smooth.

ATTACH THE BACK SLATS. Before attaching the back slats to the back frame, clamp a straight board across the fronts of the posts with its top edge 8½" up from the bottoms of the posts **(photo G).** Using this board as a guide will make it easy to keep the slats aligned as you attach them. Fasten the end slats to the back frame with glue and deck screws,

Use the first completed back slat as a template for tracing cutting lines on the rest of the back slats.

Clamp a straight board to the back frame to help keep the back slats aligned along their bottom edges as you install them.

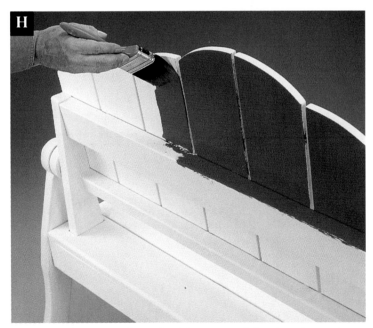

Apply two thin coats of exterior primer to seal the pine, then paint the park bench with two coats of enamel house trim paint.

making sure the bottoms are resting flat against the clamped guide board. (For more information on back slat positioning, see the *Diagram*, page 13.) Make sure the outside edges of the end slats are flush with the outside edges of the posts. Attach the remaining slats be-

tween the end slats, spaced so the gaps are even.

ASSEMBLE THE BENCH. Attach the rear frame by sliding the back into place inside the notches in the rear seat slat. The posts should rest against the back rail and side rails. Keep the bottoms of the posts

flush with the bottom edges of the side rails. Drive counterbored, 2½" screws through the posts and into the side rails, and through the back rail and into the posts to secure the rear frame to the bench seat.

APPLY FINISHING TOUCHES. Apply moisture-resistant glue to ⅜"-dia. wood plugs, and insert them into each counterbored screw hole. Sand the plugs until they are flush with the wood. Sand all surfaces smooth with medium (100 or 120 grit) sandpaper, then finish-sand the project with fine (150 or 180 grit) sandpaper. Finish as desired; we used two thin coats of primer and two coats of exterior house trim paint **(photo H).** Whenever you use untreated pine for an outdoor project, it is very important that you apply an exterior-rated finish to protect the wood. Untreated pine is susceptible to rot and other forms of moisture damage.

Firewood Shelter

Those stacks of firewood won't be an eyesore anymore once you build this ranch-style firewood shelter for your yard.

CONSTRUCTION MATERIALS

Quantity	Lumber
8	2 × 4" × 8' cedar
5	2 × 6" × 8' cedar
10	⅝ × 8" × 8' cedar lap siding

This handsome firewood shelter combines rustic ranch styling with ample sheltered storage that keeps firewood off the ground and obscured from sight. Clad on the sides and roof with beveled cedar lap siding, the shelter has the look and feel of a permanent structure. But because it is freestanding, it can be moved around as needed, and requires no time-consuming foundation work.

This firewood shelter is large enough to hold an entire face cord of firewood. And since the storage area is sheltered and raised to avoid ground contact and allow air flow, wood dries quickly and is ready to use when you need it.

OVERALL SIZE:
62" HIGH
24" DEEP
8' LONG

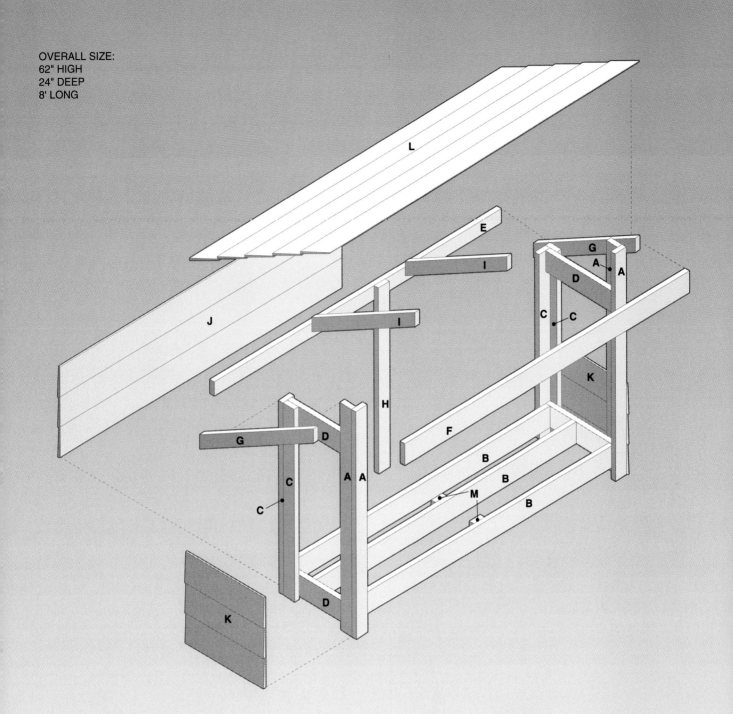

Cutting List

Key	Part	Dimension	Pcs.	Material
A	Front post	1½ × 3½ × 59"	4	Cedar
B	Bottom rail	1½ × 5½ × 82½"	3	Cedar
C	Rear post	1½ × 3½ × 50"	4	Cedar
D	End rail	1½ × 5½ × 21"	4	Cedar
E	Back rail	1½ × 3½ × 88¾"	1	Cedar
F	Front rail	1½ × 5½ × 88¾"	1	Cedar
G	Roof support	1½ × 3½ × 33¾"	2	Cedar

Cutting List

Key	Part	Dimension	Pcs.	Material
H	Middle post	1½ × 3½ × 49"	1	Cedar
I	Middle support	1½ × 3½ × 27¾"	2	Cedar
J	Back siding	⅝ × 8 × 88¾"	3	Cedar siding
K	End siding	⅝ × 8 × 24"	6	Cedar siding
L	Roof strips	⅝ × 8 × 96"	5	Cedar siding
M	Prop	1½ × 3½ × 7½"	2	Cedar

Materials: ⅜ × 3½" lag screws (24), 1½" spiral siding nails, deck screws (2½", 3"), finishing materials.

Note: Measurements reflect the actual size of dimensional lumber.

Directions: Firewood Shelter

BUILD THE FRAME. The basic framework for the firewood shelter is made of four corner posts, connected by end rails at the sides and full-width bottom rails. Cut the front posts (A) and rear posts (C). Butt the edges of the front posts together in pairs to form the corner posts. Join the post pairs with 2½" deck screws, driven through countersunk pilot holes at 8" intervals. Join the rear posts in pairs. Cut the bottom rails (B) and end rails (D). Assemble two bottom rails and two end rails into a rectangular frame,

Use a smaller bit to extend the pilot holes for the lag screws into the ends of the bottom rails.

with the end rails covering the ends of the bottom rails. Set the third bottom rail between the end rails, centered between the other bottom rails. Mark the ends of the bottom rails on the outside faces of the end rails. Drill a pair of ⅜"-dia. pilot holes for lag screws through the end rails at each bottom rail position—do not drill into the bottom rails. Drill a ¾"-dia. counterbore for each pilot hole, deep enough so the heads of the lag screws will be recessed. Drill a smaller, ¼"-dia. pilot hole through each pilot hole in the end rails, into the ends of the bottom rails **(photo A)**. Drive a ⅜ × 3½" lag screw fitted with a washer at each pilot hole, using a socket wrench. Next, draw reference lines across the inside faces of the corner posts, 2" up from the bottoms. With the corner posts upright and about 82" apart, set 2"-high spacers next to each corner post to support the frame. Position the bottom rail frame between the corner posts, and attach the frame to the corner posts by driving two 3" deck screws through the corner posts and into the outer

faces of the bottom rails. Drive a pair of ⅜ × 3½" lag screws, fitted with washers, through the sides of the corner posts and into the bottom rails—the lag screws need to go through the post and end rail, and into the end of the bottom rail, without hitting the lag screws that are already driven through the end rails. Drill counterbored pilot holes and drive the lag screws. Complete the frame by installing end rails at the tops of the corner posts, using countersunk deck screws. Make sure the tops of the end rails are flush with the tops of the rear posts **(photo B)**.

MAKE THE ROOF FRAME. The roof is made from beveled cedar lap siding that is attached to a roof frame supported by the corner posts. Cut the back rail (E), front rail (F), roof supports (G), middle post (H) and middle supports (I) to length. The roof supports and middle supports are mitered at the ends. To make cutting lines for the miter cuts, mark a point 1½" in from each end, along the edge of the board. Draw diagonal lines from each point to the opposing corner. Cut along

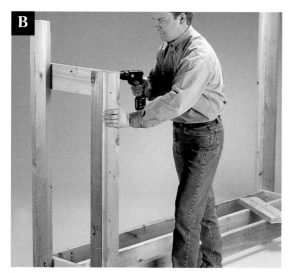

Attach end rails between front and rear corner posts.

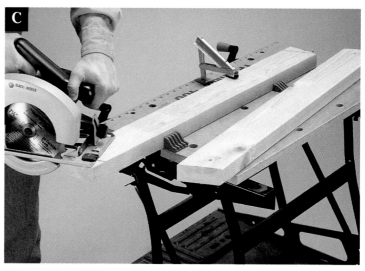

Miter-cut the middle supports and roof supports with a circular saw.

Attach the front rail by driving screws through the outer roof supports, making sure the top of the rail is flush with the tops of the supports.

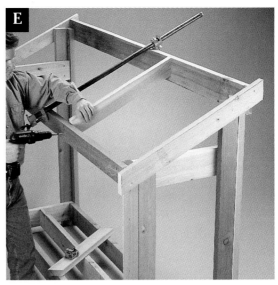

Attach the middle roof supports by driving screws through the front and back rails.

the lines with a circular saw **(photo C).** Use countersunk 3" deck screws to fasten the back rail to the backs of the rear corner posts, flush with their tops and sides. Fasten a roof support to the outsides of the corner posts, using countersunk deck screws, and making sure the top of each roof support is flush with the high point of each post end. The roof supports should overhang the posts equally in the front and rear. Use countersunk deck screws to attach the front rail between the roof supports **(photo D),** making sure the top is flush with the tops of the roof supports. Attach the middle supports between the front rail and back rail, 30" in from each rail end. Drive deck screws through the front and back rails into the ends of the middle supports **(photo E).** Use a pipe clamp to hold the supports in place as you attach them. Next, position the middle post (H) so it fits against the outside of the rear bottom rail and the inside of the top back rail. Make sure the middle post is perpen-

dicular and extends past the bottom rail by 2", and attach it with countersunk deck screws. Finally, help keep the bottom rails from sagging under the weight of the firewood by cutting a pair of 2 × 4 props (M) to length and attaching them to the front two bottom rails, aligned with the middle post. Make sure the tops of the props are flush with the tops of the bottom rails.

ATTACH THE SIDING & ROOF. Cut pieces of 8"-wide beveled cedar lap siding to length to make the siding strips (J, K) and the roof strips (L). Starting 2" up from the bottoms of the rear posts, fasten the back siding strips (J) with two 1½" siding nails driven through each strip and into the posts, near the top and bottom edge of the strip. Work your way up, overlapping each piece of siding by ½", making sure the thicker edges of the beveled siding strips are lower. Attach the end siding (K) to the corner posts, with the seams aligned with the seams in the back siding. Attach the roof strips (L) to the

Attach the roof strips with siding nails, starting at the back edge and working your way forward.

roof supports, starting at the back edge. Drive two nails into each roof support. Make sure the wide edge of the beveled siding is lower. Attach the rest of the roof strips, overlapping the strip below by about ½" **(photo F),** until you reach the front edges of the roof supports. You can leave the cedar wood untreated, or apply an exterior wood stain to keep the wood from turning gray as it weathers.

Trellis Planter

Two traditional yard furnishings are combined into one compact package.

The decorative trellis and the cedar planter are two staples found in many yards and gardens. By integrating the appealing shape and pattern of the trellis with the rustic, functional design of the cedar planter, this building project showcases the best qualities of both furnishings.

Because the 2 × 2 lattice trellis is attached to the planter, not permanently fastened to a wall or railing, the trellis planter can be moved easily to follow changing sunlight patterns, or to occupy featured areas of your yard. It is also easy to move for storage during non-growing seasons. You may even want to consider installing wheels or casters on the base for greater mobility.

Building the trellis planter is a very simple job. The trellis portion is made entirely of strips of 2 × 2 cedar, fashioned together in a crosshatch pattern. The planter bin is a basic wood box, with panel sides and a two-board bottom with drainage holes, that rests on a scalloped base. The trellis is screwed permanently to the back of the planter bin.

Stocking the trellis planter with plantings is a matter of personal taste and growing conditions. In most areas, ivy, clematis, and grapevines are good examples of climbing plants that can be trained up the trellis. Ask at your local gardening center for advice on plantings. Plants can be set into the bin in containers, or you can fill the bin with potting soil and plant directly in the bin.

CONSTRUCTION MATERIALS

Quantity	Lumber
1	2 × 6" × 8' cedar
1	2 × 4" × 6' cedar
4	2 × 2" × 8' cedar
2	1 × 6" × 8' cedar
1	1 × 2" × 6' cedar

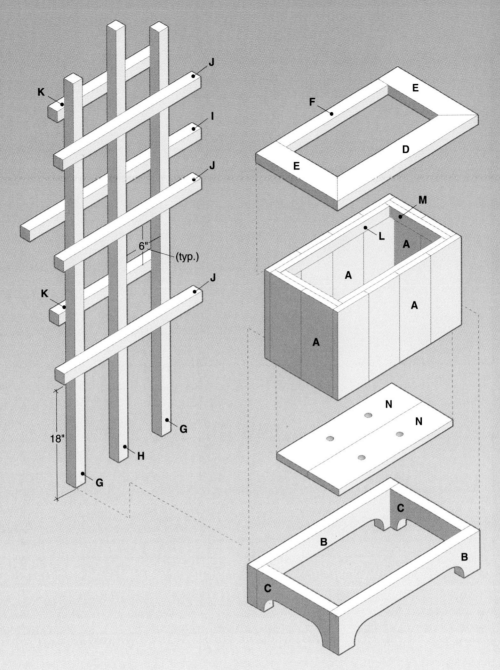

OVERALL SIZE:
65" HIGH
17¼" WIDE
25" LONG

6" (typ.)

18"

Cutting List

Key	Part	Dimension	Pcs.	Material
A	Box slat	⅞ × 5½ × 13"	12	Cedar
B	Base front/back	1½ × 5½ × 25"	2	Cedar
C	Base end	1½ × 5½ × 12¾"	2	Cedar
D	Cap front	1½ × 3½ × 25"	1	Cedar
E	Cap end	1½ × 3½ × 15¾"	2	Cedar
F	Cap back	1½ × 1½ × 18"	1	Cedar
G	End post	1½ × 1½ × 59½"	2	Cedar

Cutting List

Key	Part	Dimension	Pcs.	Material
H	Center post	1½ × 1½ × 63½"	1	Cedar
I	Long rail	1½ × 1½ × 30"	1	Cedar
J	Medium rail	1½ × 1½ × 24"	3	Cedar
K	Short rail	1½ × 1½ × 18"	2	Cedar
L	Cleat	⅞ × 1½ × 18¼"	2	Cedar
M	Cleat	⅞ × 1½ × 11"	2	Cedar
N	Bottom board	⅞ × 5½ × 20¼"	2	Cedar

Materials: Moisture-resistant wood glue, deck screws (1⅝", 2½"), finishing materials.

Note: Measurements reflect the actual size of dimensional lumber.

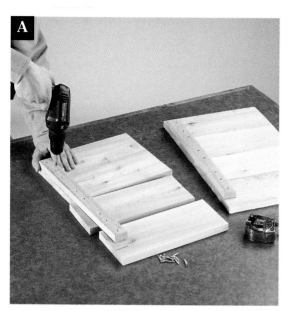

Attach the side cleats flush with the tops of the side boards.

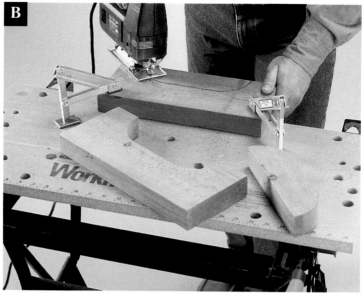

Use a jig saw to make scalloped cutouts in all four base pieces—make sure the cutouts in matching pieces are the same.

Directions: Trellis Planter

BUILD THE PLANTER BIN. The planter bin is made by attaching side panels to end panels, forming a box. Each side panel is made of four 1 × 6 cedar slats, and each end panel is made of two 1 × 6 slats. Start by cutting the box slats (A), base front and back (B), base ends (C), and cleats (L, M). Arrange the slats edge to edge in two groups of four and two groups of two, with the tops and bottoms flush in each group. Set a long cleat (L) at the top of each set of four slats, so the distance from each end of the cleat to the end of the panel is the same. Attach the cleats to the four-slat panels with 1⅝" deck screws **(photo A),** driven through the cleats and into the slats. Next, lay the short cleats (M) at the tops of the two-slat panels, and attach them to the slats the same way. Arrange all four panels into a box shape, apply moisture-resistant wood glue to the joints, and attach the panels with 1¼"

deck screws driven through the four-slat panels and into the ends of the two-slat panels.

INSTALL THE BIN BOTTOM. Cut the bottom boards (N) to length. Set the bin upside down on your worksurface, and mark reference lines on the inside faces of the panels, ⅞" in from the bottom of the bin. Insert the bottom boards into the bin, aligned with the reference lines to create a ⅞" recess (scraps of 1× cedar can be slipped beneath the bottom boards as spacers). Fasten the bottom boards by driving 1⅝" deck screws through the panels, and into the edges and ends of the bottom boards. Countersink the screwheads slightly.

BUILD THE PLANTER BASE. The planter base is a frame that wraps around the bottom of the planter bin. The frame pieces are scalloped to create feet at the corners when the frame is assembled. Begin by cutting the base front and back (B) boards and the base ends (C). To draw the contours for

the scallops on the front and back boards, set the point of a compass at the bottom edge of the base front, 5" in from one end. Set the compass to a 2½" radius, and draw a curve to mark the curved end of the cutout (see *Diagram*). Draw a straight line to connect the tops of the curves, 2½" up from the bottom of the board, to complete the scalloped cutout. Make the cutout with a jig saw, then sand any rough spots in the cut. Use the board as a template for marking a matching cutout on the base back. Draw a similar cutout on one base end, except with the point of the compass 4½" in from the ends. Cut out both end pieces with a jig saw **(photo B).** Cut the other pieces to shape. Draw reference lines for countersunk wood screws, ⁷⁄₁₆" from the ends of the base sides. Drill three evenly spaced pilot holes through the lines. Fasten the base ends between the base front and back with three evenly spaced deck screws driven at each joint.

The recess beneath the bottom boards in the planter bin provides access for driving screws.

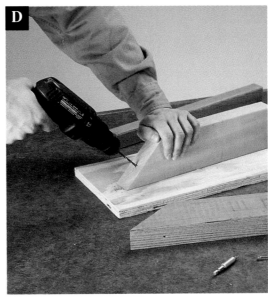

Before attaching the cap ends, drill pilot holes through the mitered ends of the cap front ends.

ATTACH THE BIN TO THE BASE. Set the base frame and planter bin on their sides. Position the planter bin inside the base so it extends ⅞" past the top of the base. Drive 1⅝" deck screws through the base and into the planter bin to secure the parts **(photo C).**

MAKE THE CAP FRAME. The top of the bin is wrapped with a wood cap. Cut the cap front (D), cap ends (E) and cap back (F) to length. Cut 45° miters at one end of each cap end, and at both ends of the cap front. Make the mitered corners by drilling pilot holes through the joints **(photo D)** and fastening them with glue and 1⅝" deck screws. Clamp the cap front and cap ends to the front of your worktable to hold them while you drive the screws. Fasten the cap back between the cap ends with wood screws, making sure the back edges are flush. Set the cap frame on the planter bin so the back edges are flush. Drill countersunk pilot holes, and drive 2½" deck screws through

the cap frame and into the side and end cleats.

MAKE THE TRELLIS. The trellis is made from pieces of 2 × 2 assembled in a crosshatch pattern. The exact number and placement of the 2 × 2 pieces is up to you—you can use the same spacing we used (see *Diagram*), or create your own. Cut the end posts (G), center post (H) and rails (I, J, K) to length. Lay the end posts and center post together side by side with their bottom edges flush, so you can gang-mark the rail positions. Use a square as a guide for drawing lines across all three posts, 18" up from the bottom. Draw the next line 7½" up from the first. Draw additional lines across the posts, spaced 7½" apart. Cut two 7"-wide scrap blocks, and use them to separate the posts as you assemble the trellis. Attach the rails to the posts in the sequence shown in the *Diagram*, using 1⅝" screws **(photo E).** Alternate from the fronts to the backs of the posts when installing the rails.

APPLY FINISHING TOUCHES. Fasten the trellis to the back of the planter bin so the bottoms of the posts rest on the top edge of the base. Drive countersunk 2½" deck screws through the posts and into the cap frame. Install a 1"-dia. spade bit in your drill, and drill a pair of drainage holes in each board (see *Diagram*, page 23). Stain the finished project as desired. We used an exterior wood stain.

Temporary spacers hold the posts in position while the trellis crossrails are attached.

Driveway Marker

An inviting yard ornament that graces the entrance to your driveway or front walk, and directs foot traffic wherever you want it to go.

CONSTRUCTION MATERIALS

Quantity	Lumber
1	2 × 4" × 8' cedar
1	2 × 2" × 6' cedar
2	1 × 6" × 8' cedar
4	1 × 2" × 8' cedar

Bestow a sense of order on your front yard by building this handsome cedar driveway marker. Position it on your lawn at the entry to your driveway to keep cars from wandering off the paved surface; or set a driveway marker on each side of your front walk to create a formal entry to your home.

This freestanding driveway marker has many benefits you'll appreciate: the fence-style slats slope away from the corner post to create a sense of flow; the broad corner post can be used to mount address numbers, making your home easier to find for visitors and in emergencies; and, behind the front slats, you'll find a spacious planter.

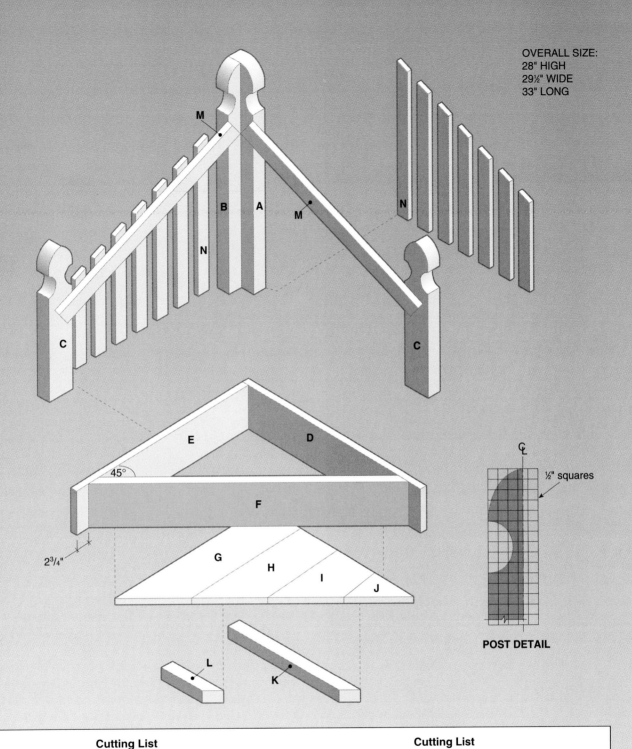

OVERALL SIZE:
28" HIGH
29½" WIDE
33" LONG

45°

2³⁄₄"

½" squares

POST DETAIL

Cutting List

Key	Part	Dimension	Pcs.	Material
A	Corner post	1½ × 3½ × 28"	1	Cedar
B	Corner post	1½ × 1½ × 28"	1	Cedar
C	End post	1½ × 3½ × 18½"	2	Cedar
D	Planter side	⅞ × 5½ × 26½"	1	Cedar
E	Planter side	⅞ × 5½ × 25½"	1	Cedar
F	Planter back	⅞ × 5½ × 33"	1	Cedar
G	Bottom board	⅞ × 5½ × 23"	1	Cedar

Cutting List

Key	Part	Dimension	Pcs.	Material
H	Bottom board	⅞ × 5½ × 17"	1	Cedar
I	Bottom board	⅞ × 5½ × 11"	1	Cedar
J	Bottom board	⅞ × 5½ × 6"	1	Cedar
K	Long cleat	1½ × 1½ × 21"	1	Cedar
L	Short cleat	1½ × 1½ × 11"	1	Cedar
M	Stringer	⅞ × 1½ × 27"	2	Cedar
N	Slat	⅞ × 1½ × 20"	14	Cedar

Materials: Moisture-resistant glue, deck screws (¼", 2", 2½"), 2" brass numbers (optional), finishing materials.

Note: Measurements reflect the actual size of dimensional lumber.

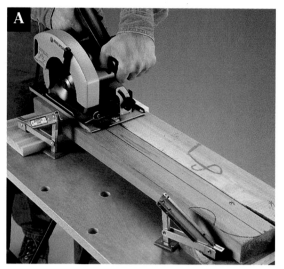

Rip the thin corner post to width with a circular saw.

Sand the top of the corner post assembly so the joint is smooth.

Lay the bin frame on the bottom boards and trace along the back inside edge to mark cutting lines.

Directions: Driveway Marker

CUT THE POSTS. This driveway marker is a freestanding yard ornament supported by single 2 × 4 posts at each end and a doubled 2 × 4 post at the corner. The tops of the posts feature French Gothic-style cutouts. Cut the corner posts (A, B) and end posts (C) to length from cedar 2 × 4. Draw a ½"-square grid pattern at the top of one of the end posts. Use the grid pattern on page 27 as a reference for drawing the top contour onto the end post. Mark a

centerpoint at the top of the post and draw the pattern as shown on one side. Reverse the pattern on the other side to create the finished shape. Use a jig saw to cut the end post to shape, then mount a drum sander attachment in your electric drill and use it to smooth out the cut. Use the shaped end post as a template to mark cutting lines at the top of the other end post. Cut and sand the other end post. To make the corner posts, mark centerpoints at the top of each corner post, then trace the contour of one end post on one side of the centerline. On one corner post, draw a line down the length of the post, 2" in from the side with no contour cutout—this will be the narrower post (B). To rip this post to width, first attach two pieces of scrap wood to your worksurface, then screw the post, facedown, to the wood scrap (making sure to drive screws in the waste area of the post). Next, butt a scrap the same thickness as the post next to the post, to use as a guide for the circular saw. Attach the guide board to the wood scraps, then set the edge

guide on the saw so it follows the outside edge of the scrap. Make the rip cut along the cutting line **(photo A).** Cut the contours at the tops of the corner posts, and sand smooth.

BUILD THE CORNER POST. The two corner post boards (A, B) are joined together to form a two-piece corner post. First, apply moisture-resistant wood glue to the ripped edge of the narrower post board (B), then lay it on the face of the wider post board (A) so the joint at the corner is flush and the tops of the contours come together in a smooth line. Drive 2½" deck screws through the wider board and into the edge of the narrower board, spaced at 4" intervals, and driven through countersunk pilot holes. After the glue sets, use a sander to smooth out the tops **(photo B).**

MAKE THE PLANTER FRAME. The planter is a triangular bin that fits in the back of the driveway marker. The bin includes a three-board frame that supports the bottom boards. Cut the planter sides (D, E) to length, making square cuts at the ends. The ends of the planter back (F) are beveled so they fit flush

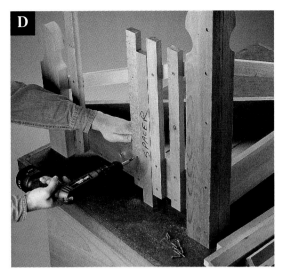

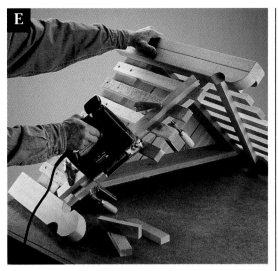

Use one slat as a spacer to set the correct gap as you fasten the slats to the bin and the stringers.

Use a cutting guide to trim the tops of the slats so they are flush with the tops of the stringers.

against the sides when the bin is formed. Set your circular saw to make a 45° cut, and cut the planter back to length, making sure the bevels both go inward from the same side (see *Diagram*). Apply glue to the ends of the planter back, then assemble the back and the sides by driving 2" deck screws through the outside faces of the side and into the ends of the back. This will create a setback of about 2¾" from the joints to the ends of the sides. Countersink the pilot holes slightly.

ATTACH THE BIN BOTTOM. Cut the bottom boards (G, H, I, J) to the full lengths indicated in the *Cutting List.* Lay the boards on your worksurface, arranged from shortest to longest, and butted together edge to edge. Set the bin frame on top of the boards so the inside edges of the frame sides are flush with the outer edges of the boards, and the bottom boards extend past the back edge of the frame. Trace along the inside of the frame back to mark cutting lines on the bottom boards **(photo C).** This should create bottom boards

that fit exactly inside the frame. Attach the bottom boards with glue and 2" deck screws driven through the frame and into the ends of the bottom boards. Make sure the bottoms of the bottom boards are flush with the bottom of the frame. Cut the long cleat (K) and short cleat (L) to size, making a 45° miter cut at one end of each cleat. Turn the planter bin upside down and attach the cleats so one is about 1½" from one of the sides, and the other is about 11½" from the same side—the cleats simply reinforce the bottom of the bin. Attach them by driving two 2" deck screws through each cleat where it meets each bottom board.

ATTACH THE BIN & POSTS. Set the bin on 2"-tall spacers, then fit the corner post assembly over the front corner of the bin and attach with glue and 1½" deck screws. Attach the end posts so each is 29½" away from the corner post assembly.

ATTACH STRINGERS & SLATS. The stringers (M) are attached between the tops of the posts to support the tops of the slats. Cut the stringers to size, and at-

tach them to the insides of the posts so the top edges are all 1½" below the bottom of the post contour at the point where the stringer meets each post. Next, cut all the slats (N) to 20" in length (the tops will be trimmed after the slats are installed). Attach them to the bin and the stringers, spaced at 1½" intervals—use one of the slats as a spacer to set the gap **(photo D).** Install all 14 slats, making sure the bottoms are flush with the bottom of the bin. Clamp a piece of 1 × 2 scrap against the outside faces of the slats to use as a cutting guide—the scrap should be directly opposite the stringer on the back side of the slats. Cut along the guide with a jig saw to trim the slats so the tops are even with the top of the stringer **(photo E).**

APPLY FINISHING TOUCHES. Sand all exposed surfaces and apply two or more coats of exterior wood stain. If your marker will be visible from the curb, you may want to attach 2"-high brass numbers to the corner post to indicate your street address.

Sundial

This throwback to ancient times casts a shadow of classical elegance in your yard or garden— and it tells time, too.

Sundials have been popular garden accessories for just about as long as there have been formal gardens. While their time-telling function is not as critical as it was around the time of the Roman Empire, sundials today continue to dot formal gardens, and even suburban flower beds, throughout the world.

The design for the cedar sundial shown here contains a few elements that harken back to ancient times. The fluted pillar suggests the famous architectural columns of Old World cathedrals and amphitheaters. The plates at the top and base

are trimmed with a Roman Ogee router bit for a Classical touch. Making these cuts requires a router and several different types of router bits. If you don't mind a little plainer look, you can bypass the router work and simply round over the parts with a power sander.

This sundial is not just another stylish accent for your yard or garden. You can actually use it to tell time. Simply mount the triangular shadowcaster (called a "gnomon") to

the face of the sundial, and orient it so it points north. Then calibrate the face at twelve hourly intervals. That way you know that the positioning of the numbers is accurate.

This sundial is secured to the ground with a post anchor that fits around a mounting block on the underside of the sundial. The anchor is driven into the ground, making it easy to move the sundial (you'll appreciate this the first time Daylight Savings Time comes around).

CONSTRUCTION MATERIALS

Quantity	Lumber
1	1 × 12" × 4' cedar
1	6 × 6" × 4' cedar
1	4 × 4" × 4' cedar

OVERALL SIZE:
39¾" HIGH
11¼" WIDE
11¼" LONG

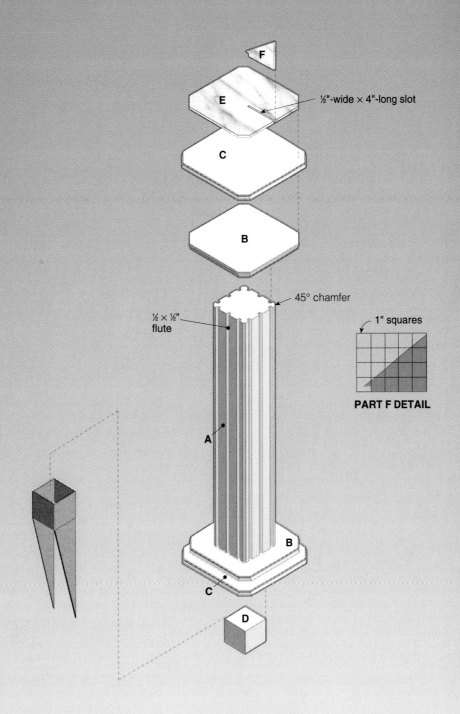

½"-wide × 4"-long slot

45° chamfer

½ × ½"
flute

1" squares

PART F DETAIL

Cutting List				
Key	**Part**	**Dimension**	**Pcs.**	**Material**
A	Column	5½ × 5½ × 32¾"	1	Cedar
B	Inner plate	⅞ × 10 × 10"	2	Cedar
C	Outer plate	⅞ × 11¼ × 11¼"	2	Cedar

Cutting List				
Key	**Part**	**Dimension**	**Pcs.**	**Material**
D	Mounting block	3½ × 3½ × 3"	1	Cedar
E	Dial face	⅜ × 10 × 10"	1	Ceramic tile
F	Gnomon	¼ × 3½ × 16½"	1	Plexiglass

Materials: 1¼", 2" galvanized deck screws, construction adhesive, silicone caulk, clock-face numbers, 4 × 4 metal post anchor.

Note: Measurements reflect the actual thickness of dimensional lumber.

Directions: Sundial

MAKE THE COLUMN. Cut the column from a 6 × 6" cedar post, then use a router to make the decorative grooves (called flutes) that run up and down the post. Start the column construction by cutting the column (A) to length from a 4'-long 6 × 6" cedar post. Next, use a combination square as a marking gauge to lay out three pairs of parallel lines lengthwise on each face of the column —the lines in each pair should be ½" apart **(photo A).** These lines form the outlines for the fluted grooves that will be cut into the post. The two outer-flute outlines should start ¾"

from the edge, and the middle flute should be 1¼" from each outer outline. Install a ½" core box bit in your router—a core box bit is a straight bit with a rounded bottom. Hook the edge guide on the foot of your router over the edge of the post (or, use a straightedge cutting guide to guide the router), and cut each ½"-deep flute in two passes. After all 12 flutes are cut, install a 45° chamfering bit in your router and trim off all four edges of the column **(photo B).**

CUT THE FLAT PARTS. Two flat, square boards are sandwiched together and attached at the top and bottom of the column. The boards are trimmed at the corners to mimic the shape of the floor tile we used for the sundial face, and they also feature decorative edges cut with a router. Cut the inner plates (B) and outer plates (C) to

size from 1 × 12 cedar. After the plates are cut to final size, trim off a corner with 1" legs from all four corners of each plate, using a jig saw **(photo C).** Install a piloted bit in your router to cut edge contours (we used a double ogee fillet bit), then cut the roundovers on all edges of the plates **(photo D).**

MAKE THE SUNDIAL FACE. We used a piece of octagonal marble floor tile for the face of our sundial. If you prefer, you can use inexpensive ceramic floor tile instead of marble, but either way you should purchase a piece of tile that is already cut to the correct size and shape for the project (cutting floor tile is very difficult). The shadow-caster, or gnomon, is cut from plexiglass, and inserted into a slot in the marble. Lay out the ¼"-wide, 4"-long slot for the gnomon, centered on one edge of the sundial face. Have the slot cut at a tile shop (if this is a problem, you are probably better off eliminating the slot than trying to cut it yourself). Next, mark a 1"-square grid pattern on a small piece of ¼"-thick white plexiglass. Lay out the shape and dimensions of the gnomon,

Lay out three ½"-wide flutes on each column face using a combination square as a marking gauge.

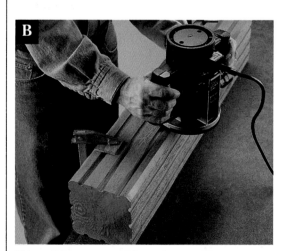

Trim off the corners of the column with a router and a 45° chamfering bit.

Cut triangular cutoffs with 1" legs at each corner of each plate.

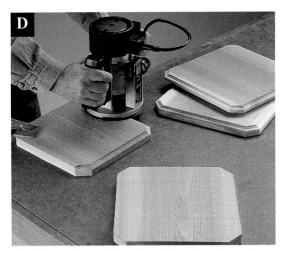

Cut decorative profiles along the edges of the inner and outer plates.

Make sure screws driven through the outer plate are at least 2" in from the edges.

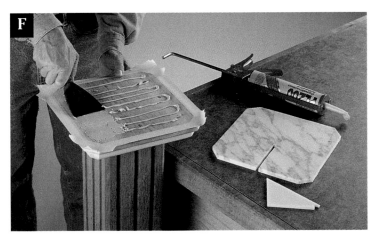

Frame the top of the top outer plate with masking tape, then apply a layer of construction adhesive to attach the sundial face.

following the *Grid Pattern* (F) on page 31. Mount a wood-cutting blade with medium-size teeth in your jig saw, and cut the gnomon shape. Sand the edges with 100-grit sandpaper, then finish-sand with fine paper, up to 180-or 220-grit. Fit the gnomon into the slot on the sundial face.

ASSEMBLE THE SUNDIAL. Attach an inner plate, centered, to each end of the column, using 2½" deck screws. Cut the mounting block (D) to length from 4 × 4 cedar (or two pieces of cedar 2 × 4). Attach the block to one face of the bottom outer plate, centered, using

deck screws driven through the plate and into the block. Do not attach the base plate to the column assembly yet. Attach the top outer plate to the top inner plate, making sure the overhang is equal on all four sides and the corners align **(photo E).** Set the post on its base, and attach the sundial face to the top outer plate, using construction adhesive **(photo F).** Make sure the face is centered and in alignment. Place construction adhesive into the gnomon slot, then insert the gnomon into the slot and press firmly. Seal all joints around the edges of the gnomon and the edges of the

face, using clear silicone caulk. Attach the bottom outer plate by laying the column on its side and driving 1¼" deck screws up through the outer plate and into the inner plate. Coat wood parts with exterior wood stain.

INSTALL & CALIBRATE THE SUN-DIAL. Choose a sunny spot to install your sundial. Lay a piece of scrap wood on the spot, pointing directly north (use a magnetic compass for reference). Purchase a metal post anchor for a 4 × 4 post (most have an attached metal stake about 18" long). Drive the post anchor (G) into the ground at the desired location, making sure one side of the box part of the anchor is perpendicular to the scrap piece facing north. Insert the mounting block on the base of the post into the anchor, making sure the gnomon is facing north. To calibrate the sundial, mark a point at the edge of the shadow from the gnomon at the top of every hour. Apply hour markers at those points. We used metal Roman numerals from a craft store, attached with clear silicone caulk.

Yard & Garden Cart

*With a 4 cu. ft. bin and a built-in rack for long-handled tools, this
sleek yard-and-garden cart is hardworking and versatile.*

CONSTRUCTION MATERIALS

Quantity	Lumber
1	2 × 6" × 8' cedar
5	2 × 4" × 8' cedar
2	1 × 6" × 8' cedar
2	1 × 4" × 8' cedar
1	1"-dia. × 3' dowel

This sturdy yard-and-garden cart picks up where a plain wheelbarrow leaves off. It includes many clever features to make doing yard work more efficient, without sacrificing hauling space in the bin area.

The notches in the handle frame do double duty as a rack that keeps long-handled tools stable as you rumble across the yard. The handle itself folds down and locks in place like a kickstand when the cart is parked, then flips up to form an extra-long handle that takes advantage of simple physics to make the cart easier to push and steer. And because it's made of wood, this cart will never become rusty or full of dents.

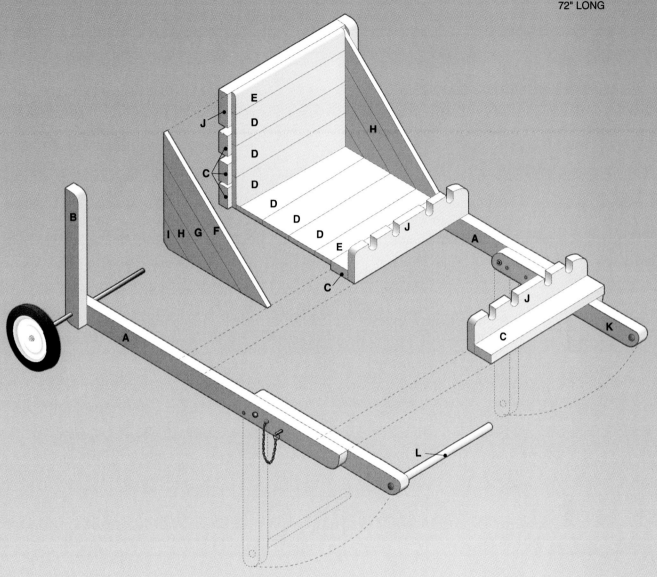

Cutting List

Key	Part	Dimension	Pcs.	Material
A	Back support	1½ × 3½ × 57"	2	Cedar
B	Front support	1½ × 3½ × 23½"	2	Cedar
C	Cross rail	1½ × 3½ × 24"	5	Cedar
D	Bin slat	⅞ × 5½ × 22½"	6	Cedar
E	End slat	1½ × 3½ × 22½"	2	Cedar
F	Bin side	⅞ × 3½ × 28"	2	Cedar

Cutting List

Key	Part	Dimension	Pcs.	Material
G	Bin side	⅞ × 3½ × 21"	2	Cedar
H	Bin side	⅞ × 3½ × 14"	2	Cedar
I	Bin side	⅞ × 3½ × 7"	8	Cedar
J	Top rail	1½ × 5½ × 24"	3	Cedar
K	Arm	1½ × 3½ × 32"	2	Cedar
L	Handle	1"-dia. × 21"	1	Dowel

Materials: Deck screws (2", 2½"), 4d finish nails (2), 10" utility wheels (2), steel axle rod (30"), ³⁄₁₆"-dia. cotter pins, ⅜"-dia. hitch pins and chain (2), finishing materials.

Note: Measurements reflect the actual size of dimensional lumber.

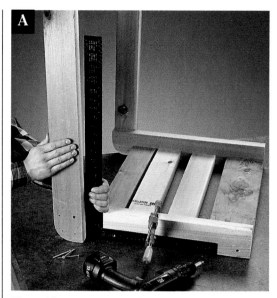

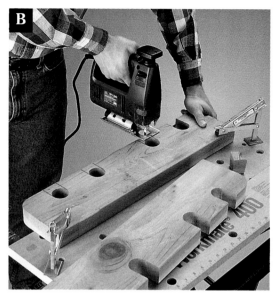

Test with a square to make sure the front supports and back supports are joined at right angles.

Make straight cuts from the edge of each rail to the sides of the holes to make the tool notches.

Directions:
Yard & Garden Cart

BUILD THE CART FRAME. The frame of the cart consists of a pair of L-shaped 2 × 4 assemblies joined together by rails. Start by cutting the back supports (A), front supports (B), three cross rails (C) and one of the top rails (J). Use a compass to draw a curve with a 3½" radius on each end of the back supports and on one end of each front support. When the curves are cut, the ends of these parts will have one rounded corner and one square corner. Cut the curves with a jig saw and sand out any rough spots or saw marks. Position the top rail between the tops of the front supports (the

ends that are square at both corners). Fasten the rail between the supports with glue and 2½"deck screws driven through pilot holes (countersink all pilot holes in this project so the screw heads are recessed). Next, position two cross rails between the front supports, 9" and 14" down from the tops of the front supports. Make sure the cross rails are aligned with the top rail, and attach them with glue and deck screws. Fasten another cross rail between the bottom ends of the front supports; the bottom edge of the cross rail is 3½" up from the bottoms of the front supports and aligned with the other rails. Glue and screw the front supports to the back supports, using a square to make sure the parts are joined at right angles **(photo A)**. The unshaped ends of the back supports should be flush with the front and bottom edges of the front supports, and the back supports should be attached to the inside faces of the front supports. Drill cen-

tered, ½"-dia. holes for the wheel axles through the bottoms of the front supports and back supports, 1¾" in from the inside corner where the front and back supports are joined.

CUT THE NOTCHED TOP RAILS. Cut the two remaining top rails (J). These rails contain notches that are aligned to create a rack for tool handles. Before cutting the tool notches into the rails, use a compass to draw 1½"-radius roundover curves at each end along one side of each rail. Cut the roundovers with a jig saw. To make the tool notches in the top rails, first draw a reference line 1½" in from the rail edge between the roundovers. Mark four drilling points on the line, 3¾" and 8¼" in from each end. Use a drill and a spade bit to drill 1½"-dia. holes through the drilling points on each rail. Use a square to draw cutting lines from the sides of the holes to the near edge of each rail. Cut along the lines with a jig saw to complete the tool notches **(photo B)**.

TIP

If you need to round over the end of a board, one easy solution that gets good results is to use your belt sander like a bench grinder. Simply mount the belt sander to a worksurface sideways, so the belt is perpendicular to the worksurface and has room to spin. Turn on the sander, lay your workpiece on the worksurface, and grind away.

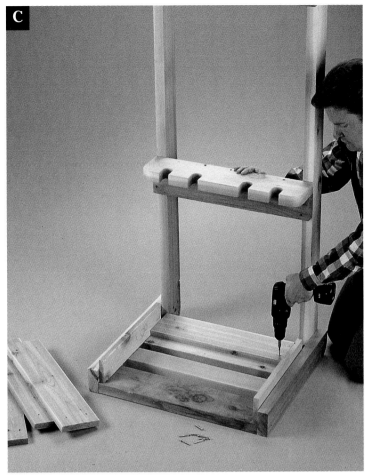

C

Attach the bin slats to the front supports, leaving a ⅛"-wide gap at both ends of each slat.

ATTACH RAILS BETWEEN THE BACK SUPPORTS. Cut two cross rails (C) and lay them flat on your worksurface. Attach a top rail to the edges of each cross rail, so the ends are flush and the edges of the top rails with the tool notches are facing up. Use 2½" deck screws driven at 4" intervals through the top rails and into the edges of the cross rails. Then set one of the assemblies on the free ends of the back supports, flush with the edges. The free edge of the cross rail should be flush with the ends of the back supports. Attach the cross rail with deck screws driven down into the back support. Attach the other rail assembly to the top edges of the back supports so the top rail faces the other rail assembly, and the free edge of the cross rail is 21" from the front ends of the back supports. This completes the assembly of the cart frame.

ATTACH THE BIN SLATS. The bin portion of the yard-and-garden cart is formed by cedar slats that are attached to the cart frame. Start by cutting the bin slats (D) and end slats (E) to size. Position one end slat and three bin slats between the front supports, with the end slat flush with the edge of the front cross rail and the last bin slat butted against the back supports. There should be a ⅞" gap between each end of each slat and the front supports. Attach the slats with glue and 2" deck screws driven down through the slats and into the cross rails **(photo C).** Fasten the rest of the bin slats to the top edges of the back supports, with a ⅞" recess at each end. Start with the slat that fits at the bottom of the bin, and work your way up, driving screws down into the tops of the back supports. Fasten the final end slat so it fits between the last bin slat and the lower cross rail on the back supports. Use a grinder or belt sander with a coarse belt to round over the front edges of the front end slat and front supports **(photo D).**

ATTACH THE BIN SIDES. The bin sides fill in the V-shape between the front and back supports. They fit into the recess created between the bin slats and the front supports. First, square-cut the bin sides (F, G, H, I) to the lengths shown in the *Cutting List* on page 35. Then, draw a miter-cutting line at each end of each bin side. Make the miter cuts with a circular saw and straightedge, or with a power miter saw if you have one. Fit the short, V-shaped sides into the openings at the sides of the bin, and attach them to the front supports with 2" deck screws. Install the rest of the bin sides in the correct order **(photo E).**

Round over the tips of the front supports and the front edge of the end slat, using a belt sander.

Fasten the bin sides in a V-shape with glue and deck screws.

Drill a pilot hole through each arm and into the ends of the handle, then drive a 4d finish nail into the hole to secure the handle.

MAKE THE ARMS. The arms (K) serve a double purpose. First, they support the handles when you wheel the cart. Second, they drop down and lock in place to support the cart in an upright position. Cut the arms (K) to length. Mark the center of each end of each arm, measuring from side to side. Measure down 3½" from each centerpoint, and mark a point. Set the point of a com-pass at each of these points, and draw a 1¾"-radius semicircle at each end of both arms. Cut the curves with a jig saw. Then drill a 1"-dia. hole for the han-dle dowel at one of the center-points on each arm. At the other centerpoint, drill a ⅜"-dia. guide hole for a carriage bolt.

ATTACH THE ARMS. The arms are attached with carriage bolts to the back supports. Drill ⅜"-dia. holes for carriage bolts through each back support, 19" from the handle end, and cen-tered between the top and bot-tom edges of the supports. Insert a ⅜"-dia. × 4"-long car-riage bolt through the outside of each ⅜"-dia. hole in the back supports. Slip a washer over each bolt, then slip the arms over the carriage bolts. Slip an-other washer over the end of each bolt, then secure the arms to the supports by tightening a lock nut onto each bolt. Do not overtighten the lock nut—the arms need to be loose enough that they can pivot freely. Cut the handle (L) to length from a 1"-dia. dowel (preferably hard-wood). Slide it into the 1"-dia. holes in the ends of the arms. Secure the handle by drilling pilot holes for 4d finish nails through each arm and into the dowel **(photo F),** then driving a finish nail into the dowel at each end.

ATTACH THE WHEELS. The wheels for the cart are 10"-dia. utility wheels fitted over a steel axle rod, and locked in place

Secure the wheels by inserting a cotter pin into a hole at the end of each axle, then bending down the arms of the pin with pliers.

with cotter pins. The wheels and steel axle rod can be purchased at a hardware store (make sure to buy an axle rod that fits the holes in the hubs of the wheels). Cut the axle rod to 30" in length with a hacksaw, and deburr it with a file or a bench grinder. (Rough-grit sandpaper will also work, but it takes longer and is hard on the hands.) Secure the axle rod in a vise, or clamp it to your worksurface, and use a steel twist bit to drill a $\frac{3}{16}$"-dia. hole $\frac{1}{8}$" in from each end of the axle. Slip the the axle through the $\frac{1}{2}$"-dia. holes drilled at the joints between the front and back supports, then slide two washers over the ends of the axles. Slip a wheel over each axle, add two washers, then insert a $\frac{3}{16}$"-dia. cotter pin into each of the holes drilled at the ends of the axle. Secure the wheels by bending down the ends of the cotter pins with a pair of pliers **(photo G).**

LOCK THE ARMS IN PLACE. On a flat surface, fold down the arm/handle assembly so the arms are perpendicular to the ground. Drill a $\frac{3}{8}$"-dia. guide hole through each back support, 1" below the carriage bolt that attaches the arms to the supports. Extend the holes all the way through the arms **(photo H).** Insert a $\frac{3}{8}$"-dia. hitch pin (or hinge pins will

do) into each hole to secure the arms. To prevent losing the pins when you remove them, attach them to the back supports with a chain or a piece of cord. Now, remove the pins and lift the arms up so they are level with the tops of the back supports. Drill $\frac{3}{8}$"-dia. holes through the arms and back supports, about 12" behind the first pin holes, for locking the arms in the cart-pushing position.

APPLY FINISHING TOUCHES. Smooth out all the sharp edges on the cart with a sander. Also sand the surfaces slightly. Apply two coats of exterior wood stain to the wood for protection. Squirt some penetrating/lubricating oil or teflon lubricant onto the axles on each side of each wheel to reduce friction.

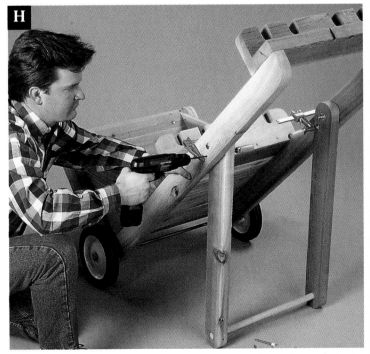

Drill $\frac{3}{8}$"-dia. holes through the back supports and into the arms for inserting the hitch pins that lock the arms in position.

Backyard Fire Pit

*Bring backwoods intimacy into your backyard
with this raised campfire pit.*

You don't have to live at the beach or on a farm to enjoy the charm of an open campfire. In many areas, small open fires are allowed in backyards if you follow guidelines for size and notification.

This backyard campfire pit is an attractive structure that lets you build backyard campfires without scarring your backyard with a permanent fire pit. Because the concrete pavers that frame the pit area are loose-laid, they can be unstacked easily so you can move the fire pit out of the way when it is not in use. Two layers of cement-board serve as a firestop at the base of the pit. To build matching seating for your fire pit, see the plans for fire pit benches on pages 44 to 47.

NOTE: Regulations regarding open fires vary greatly. Check with your local Fire Department for policies and restrictions. One rule for open fires within city limits is that they can be no larger than 3' in diameter at the base, and must be at least 20' from a permanent structure. In some areas, you are required to notify Fire Department officials prior to building an open fire. Other restrictions may apply. Always use sound safety practices, and keep a fire extinguisher handy.

CONSTRUCTION MATERIALS

Quantity	Lumber
3	1 × 4" × 8' cedar
6	2 × 2" × 8' cedar
8	2 × 4" × 8' cedar
2	⅜" × 3 × 5' cementboard

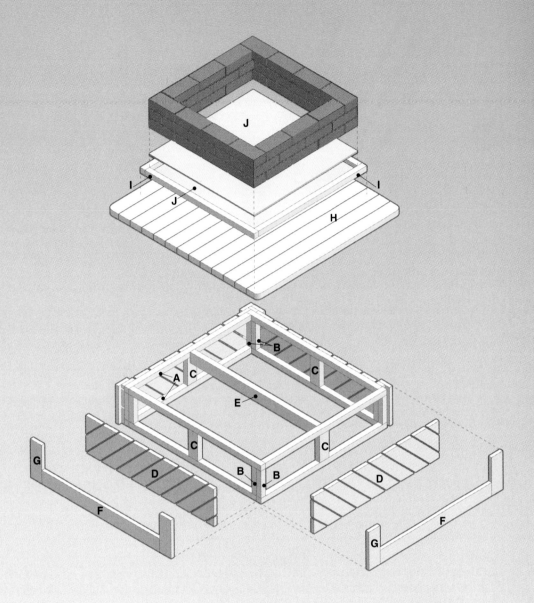

Cutting List

Key	Part	Dimension	Pcs.	Material
A	Frame side	1½ × 1½ × 42"	8	Cedar
B	Frame end	1½ × 1½ × 7½"	8	Cedar
C	Stud	1½ × 3½ × 7½"	4	Cedar
D	End slats	⅞ × 1½ × *	22	Cedar
E	Joist	1½ × 3½ × 39"	1	Cedar

Cutting List

Key	Part	Dimension	Pcs.	Material
F	Bottom trim	⅞ × 3½ × *	4	Cedar
G	Side trim	⅞ × 3½ × 10½"	8	Cedar
H	Deck slat	1½ × 3½ × 48"	13	Cedar
I	Retainer	1½ × 1½ × 36"	4	Cedar
J	Firestop	⅝ × 34½ × 34½"	2	Cementboard

Materials: Galvanized deck screws (1½", 2½"), 3 × 8" concrete pavers (48)

Note: Measurements reflect the actual size of dimensional lumber.
*Cut to fit

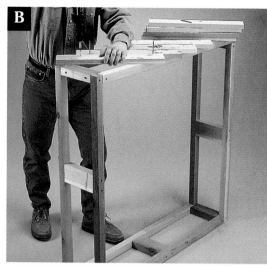

Build four 2 × 2 frames, then join them together to make the large frame that supports the fire pit deck.

Fasten the slats to the frames with deck screws, using 16d nails for spacing between each end slat.

Directions:
Backyard Fire Pit

BUILD THE FRAME. The frame sections are the first to be built on the fire pit. The slats, trim and joist are all attached to this supporting frame. Start by cutting the frame sides (A) and frame ends (B) to length from 2 × 2 cedar. Place the frame ends between the frame sides and fasten them with 2½" deck screws **(photo A).** Assemble the remaining frame ends and frame sides. Cut the studs (C) to length from 2 × 4 cedar and fasten them between the frame sides, centered between the frame ends. Fasten the frames together by driving 2½" deck screws through one frame end and into another.

FASTEN THE END SLATS. The cedar end slats are mounted diagonally on the frames and can be cut at an angle by using a circular saw and straightedge cutting guide (or a power miter box). Lay the frames on a flat surface and draw a 45° layout line across the frames, 3½" in from the frame corner. Next, cut the end slats (D) from 1 × 4

cedar and fasten them to the frames with 1½" deck screws, starting along the layout line and using 16d nails for spacing between each of the individual slats **(photo B).** Cut the slats in length so they overhang the frame edges by at least 1" on both ends. When all end slats are fastened to the frame, measure the precise end-slat overhang on each side of the frame and mark the overhang distance, two marks per frame side, on the top surfaces of the end slats. Draw a line around

the perimeter of each frame to connect the overhang marks on the end slats. Cut off the overhang on each frame side using a circular saw and a straightedge cutting guide **(photo C).** The cuts should be flush with the edges of the frame ends and sides. Be careful not to cut into the frame ends or sides, or into the deck screws fastening the end frames or end slats.

ATTACH THE JOIST & TRIM. Once the frame units have been assembled with end slats,

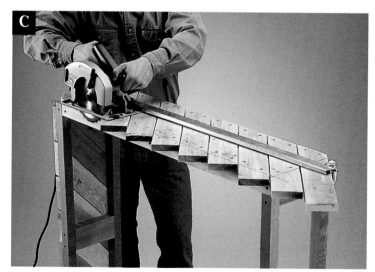

Cut off the slat overhang on each frame side using a circular saw and straightedge cutting guide.

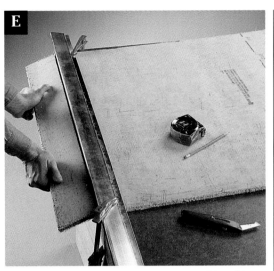

Cut roundover curves at the corners of the outside deck slats, using a jig saw.

Cut cementboard to size by scoring and breaking to make the firestop.

the joist and trim are the next items to be fastened to the frames and slats. They provide structural support for the frame and a decorative cover for the end slats. Start by cutting the joist (E) to length from 2 × 4 cedar. Mount the joist between two of the studs, flush with the top edge of the frame side, using 3½" deck screws. Next, cut the bottom trim (F) and side trim (G) pieces to length from 1 × 4 cedar. Fasten them to the end slats around the perimeter of each frame with 1½" deck screws. Be sure to overlap the side trim, then cut the bottom trim to fit between the side trim pieces.

MAKE & ATTACH THE DECK SLATS. The deck slats tie the frame units together and provide a support surface for the fire pit. Cut the deck slats (H) to length from 2 × 4 cedar and position them on the frame and across the joist, leaving an equal overhang on all sides and ⁵⁄₁₆" spacing between the slats. Fasten the slats to the frame and joist with 2½" deck screws. Draw roundover lines with a 1½" radius on the out-

side deck slats, using a compass (or by tracing a 3"-dia. can). Cut the radius corners using a jig saw **(photo D)**, then smooth the rounded corners with a power sander.

DRY-SET THE PIT SURROUND. Before you make the parts for the pit, arrange your bricks or pavers in the pattern you plan to use for the pit surround. Because brick and paver sizes vary, the dimensions of the cementboard base and retainer frame may need to be adjusted to accommodate the finished dimensions of the surround. We used standard 3 × 8" concrete pavers (actual size is 2⅝" × 7⅝") to build the surround, which is reflected in the dimensions for the retainer and firestop that are listed in the *Cutting List* on page 41. However you stack the pavers or fire bricks, make sure the surround walls are at least 7" high, with an inside diameter of 3' or less.

BUILD THE RETAINER & FIRESTOP. Cut the retainers (I) to length from 2 × 2 cedar, using the adjusted length to fit your surround, if needed. Assemble the retainer strips into a

TIP

Cementboard is a cement-based material that is used in areas exposed to moisture, most often as an underlayment for ceramic tile. It is usually sold in 3 × 5 sheets. To cut cementboard, score along the cutting line several times with a utility knife, then position the cementboard over a piece of scrap wood and break it along the line (the same way you cut wallboard).

frame to wrap the surround, using 2½" deck screws. Measure the inside dimensions of the frame, and cut two pieces of ⅝"-thick cementboard to that size using a straightedge cutting guide and a sharp utility knife **(photo E)**.

APPLY FINISHING TOUCHES. Sand the fire pit, then apply exterior wood stain to all exposed surfaces. When the stain has dried, center the retainer frame on the deck slats and place the layers of firestop into the retainer frame. Dry-lay your paver or brick surround walls inside the retainer frame, using the same pattern you dry-fit earlier. To move the backyard fire pit, or to clean the pit area, simply unstack the pavers or bricks.

Fire Pit Bench

Designed to match the Backyard Fire Pit shown on the previous pages, this versatile bench will be at home anywhere in your yard.

CONSTRUCTION MATERIALS

Quantity	Lumber
2	2 × 2" × 8' cedar
4	1 × 4" × 8' cedar
4	2 × 4" × 8' cedar
1	1 × 2" × 8' cedar

Summer cookouts, moonlit bonfires or even a midwinter warm-up are all perfect occasions to use this cedar fire pit bench, designed to accompany our Backyard Fire Pit (pages 40 to 43). If you are extremely ambitious, you can build four benches to surround the fire pit on all sides. If you don't need that much seating, build only two and arrange them to form a cozy conversation area around the fire. Even without a fire pit, you can build a single bench as a stand-alone furnishing for your favorite spot in your yard or garden.

This solid cedar bench will seat up to three adults comfortably. The slats below give the bench strength, while providing a convenient spot for storing and drying firewood.

OVERALL SIZE:
18" HIGH
18½" WIDE
48" LONG

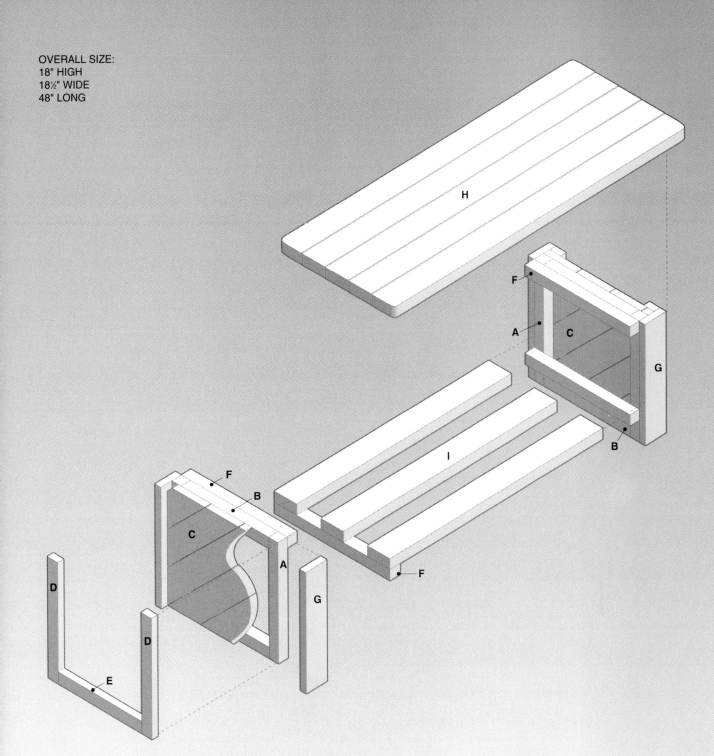

Cutting List

Key	Part	Dimension	Pcs.	Material
A	Frame side	1½ × 1½ × 16½"	4	Cedar
B	Frame end	1½ × 1½ × 14"	4	Cedar
C	End slat	⅞ × 3½ × *	12	Cedar
D	End trim	⅞ × 1½ × 15"	4	Cedar
E	Bottom trim	⅞ × 1½ × 17"	2	Cedar

Cutting List

Key	Part	Dimension	Pcs.	Material
F	Cleat	1½ × 1½ × 17"	4	Cedar
G	Side trim	⅞ × 3½ × 16½"	4	Cedar
H	Seat slat	1½ × 3½ × 48"	5	Cedar
I	Shelf slat	1½ × 3½ × 35"	3	Cedar

* Cut to fit

Materials: Galvanized deck screws (1½", 2½").

Note: Measurements reflect the actual size of dimensional lumber.

Fasten the frame sides to the frame ends with 2½" galvanized deck screws.

Trim off the ends of the slats so the ends are flush with the outside edges of the end frames.

Directions: Fire Pit Bench

BUILD THE END FRAMES. The seat slats are supported by 2×2 frames at the ends of the bench. To make the end frames, cut the frame sides (A) and frame ends (B) to length. Place a frame end between two frame sides, and fasten them together with 2½" deck screws driven through countersunk pilot holes in the frame sides and into the ends of the frame end **(photo A).** Attach another frame end between the free ends of the frame sides, then build the second end frame.

ATTACH THE END SLATS. The end slats are mounted at 45° angles to the end frames. The easiest way to cut the angles is to cut the slats so they overhang the outsides of the frame, attach all the slats, then trim them flush with a single cut along each side. Start by laying the frames on a flat surface. Use a combination square as a guide for drawing a reference line at a 45° angle to one corner on each frame, starting 3½" in from the corner. To measure and cut the end slats (C), lay

Use shelf slats to set the correct distance between the end-frame assemblies, then attach the end frames to the bottoms of the seat slats.

the end of a full-length 1×4 cedar board across one frame so one edge meets the corner and the other edge follows the reference line. Position the board so the end overhangs the frame by an inch or two, then mark a point with an equal overhang on the other side of the frame. Cut the 1×4 at this point, then fasten the cut-off piece to the frame with pairs of 1½" deck screws driven into the

end frame. Lay the 1×4 back across the frame, butted up against the attached slat, and mark and cut another slat the same way. Attach the slat, and continue cutting and attaching the rest of the slats to cover the frame. Attach slats to the other end frame. Then, draw straight cutting lines on the tops of the slats, aligned with the outside edges of the end frames. Using a straightedge and a circular

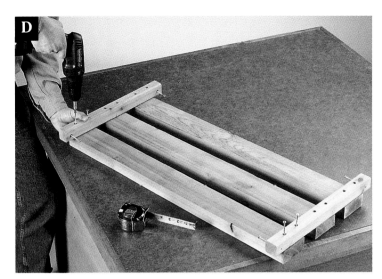

Fasten the bottom cleats to the shelf slats, keeping the ends of the slats flush with the outside edges of the cleats.

Attach the bottom cleats to the end frames with deck screws. Use a spacer to keep the cleat 1½" up from the bottom of the bench.

saw, trim off the ends of the slats along the cutting lines **(photo B).**

COMPLETE THE END FRAMES. Cut the end trim (D) and bottom trim (E) pieces from 1 × 2 cedar, and fasten them to the outside faces of the end slats so they create a frame the same length and width as the end frame. Cut the side trim (G) pieces from 1 × 4 cedar and fasten to the frame assembly with

1½" deck screws, making sure the edges of the side trim are flush with the outside edges of the end frames and trim frames. Cut the cleats (F), and fasten a top cleat to the inside of each frame with 2½" deck screws. The top cleats should be flush with the tops of the end frames (the bottom cleats will be attached later).

ATTACH THE SEAT SLATS. Start by cutting the seat slats (H) to

length from 2 × 4 cedar. Lay the seat slats on a flat surface with the ends flush and ⅛" spaces between slats. Cut the shelf slats (I). Set the end frame assemblies on top of the seat slats, then slip two of the shelf slats between the ends to set the correct distance. Fasten the end-frame assemblies to the seat slats with 1½" deck screws driven through the cleats on the end frames **(photo C).**

ATTACH THE SHELF SLATS. Arrange the shelf slats on your worksurface so the ends are flush, with 1½" gaps between the slats. Lay the remaining two cleats across the ends of the slats, and fasten the cleats to the slats with 2½" deck screws **(photo D).** Set the shelf assembly between the ends of the bench, resting on a 1½" spacer. Attach the shelf by driving deck screws through the cleats and into the end frames **(photo E).**

APPLY FINISHING TOUCHES. Use a compass to draw a 1½"-radius roundover at the corners of the seat. Cut the roundovers with a jig saw. Sand the entire fire pit bench, paying special attention to the edges of the seat slats to eliminate any possibility of slivers—as an option, you can use a router with roundover bit to trim off the sharp edges. Apply exterior wood stain to all exposed surfaces (try to match the finish of the backyard fire pit, if you are building both pieces of the fire pit set).

TIP

When storing firewood, it is tempting to cover the wood with plastic tarps to keep it dry. But more often than not, tarps will only trap moisture and keep the firewood permanently damp. With good ventilation wood dries out quickly, so your best bet is to store it uncovered or in an open shelter.

Trash Can Corral

*This two-sided structure keeps trash cans out of sight
but accessible from the curb or alley.*

CONSTRUCTION MATERIALS

Quantity	Lumber
3	2 × 4" × 8' cedar
3	2 × 2" × 8' cedar
1	1 × 8" × 6' cedar
10	1 × 6" × 8' cedar
8	1 × 4" × 8' cedar

Nothing can ruin a view from a favorite window like the sight of a dirty trash can—especially as garbage collection day draws near. With this trash can corral, you'll see a lovely, freestanding cedar fence instead of those unsightly garbage cans.

The two fence-style panels support one another, so you don't need to set fence posts in the ground or in concrete. And because the collars at the bases of the posts can be adjusted, you can position the can corral on uneven or slightly sloping ground. The staggered panel slats obstruct vision completely, but still allow air to pass through for much-needed ventilation.

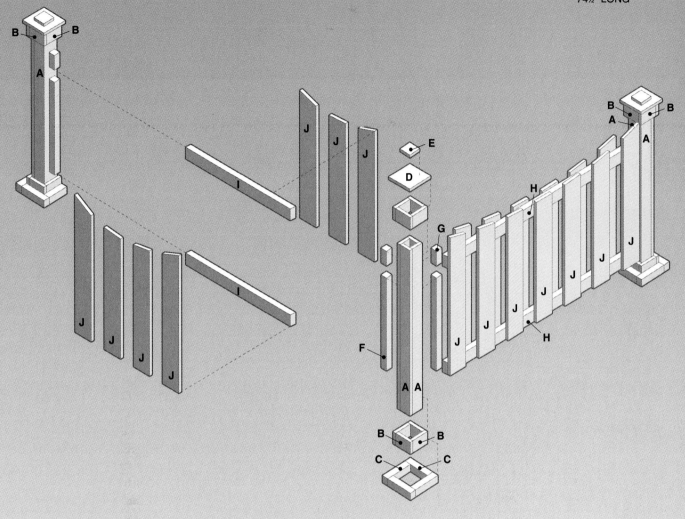

OVERALL SIZE:
50" HIGH
58" WIDE
74½" LONG

Cutting List

Key	Part	Dimension	Pcs.	Material
A	Post board	⅞ × 3½ × 48"	12	Cedar
B	Collar strip	⅞ × 3½ × 5¼"	24	Cedar
C	Foot strip	1½ × 1½ × 7½"	12	Cedar
D	Collar top	⅞ × 7¼ × 7¼"	3	Cedar
E	Collar cap	⅞ × 3½ × 3½"	3	Cedar

Cutting List

Key	Part	Dimension	Pcs.	Material
F	Long post cleat	1½ × 1½ × 26⅞"	4	Cedar
G	Short post cleat	1½ × 1½ × 4"	4	Cedar
H	Short stringer	1½ × 3½ × 35½"	2	Cedar
I	Long stringer	1½ × 3½ × 66"	2	Cedar
J	Slat	⅞ × 5½ × 40"	20	Cedar

Materials: Deck screws (1½", 2"), finishing materials.

Note: Measurements reflect the actual size of dimensional lumber.

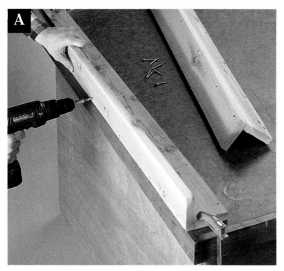

The post is made from four edge-joined boards.

Fit the top post collars onto each post and fasten them.

Attach the short post cleats 3⅝" up from the tops of the long post cleats. The top stringers on the panels fit between the cleats when installed.

Directions: Trash Can Corral

BUILD THE POSTS. Each post is made of four boards butted together to form a square. Cut the post boards (A) to length. After sanding the parts, clamp one post board on your work-surface, and butt another post board against it at a right angle. With the ends flush, attach the post boards with 2" deck screws, driven through counter-sunk pilot holes at 8" intervals **(photo A).** Repeat this process until all the post boards are fas-tened together in pairs, then fasten the pairs together to form the three posts.

MAKE & ATTACH THE COLLARS. Each post is wrapped at the top and bottom by a four-piece col-lar. The top collars each have a two-piece flat cap, and the base collars are wrapped with 1 × 2 strips for stability. Cut the collar strips (B), collar tops (D) and collar caps (E) to size. Join the collar strips together to form square frames, using 1½" deck screws. Center each col-lar cap on top of a collar top, and attach it with 1½" deck screws. Then, cover three of the frames with the tops and at-tach them with countersunk 1½" deck screws driven through the tops and into the top edges of the frames, completing the top collars. Slip a top collar over one end of each post, and drive countersunk, 1½" deck screws through the collars to secure them to the posts **(photo B).** Attach the three open frames to the other ends of the posts, with the bottom edges flush, then cut the foot strips (C) to length. Lay the foot strips together so they form frames around the bottoms of the base collars, and screw them together through each strip and into the end of the strip next to it. Make sure the bottoms of the frames are flush with the bottoms of the base collars, then attach the frames to the collars.

ATTACH THE CLEATS & SUPPORTS. The long and short post cleats (F, G) are attached to the posts to fit between and above the stringers that form the horizontal support for the corral panels. Cut the post cleats to length. Center a long post cleat side to side on one face of each post and attach it with 2" deck screws so the bot-tom of the cleat is 4⅛" above the bottom of the base collar on each post. On one of the posts, fasten another long post cleat on an adjacent post face, 4⅛" up from the bottom collar (this post will be the corner post). Center the short post cleats side to side on the same post faces as the long cleats, 3⅝" up from the tops of the long post cleats. Attach the short post cleats to the posts, making sure they are aligned with the long cleats **(photo C).**

Use 4½"-wide spacers to set the gaps between panel slats.

Use a flexible guide to mark the top contours.

BUILD THE FENCE PANELS. The two fence panels are built the same way. Start by cutting the short stringers (H), long stringers (I) and slats (J). Position the short stringers on your worksurface so they are parallel and separated by a 26⅞" gap. Attach a slat at both ends of the stringers, so the ends of the stringers are flush with the outside edges of the slats. Drive one 1½" deck screw through each slat and into the face of each stringer. Measure diagonally from corner to corner to make sure the fence panel is square. If the measurements are equal, the fence is square. If the measurements are not equal, apply pressure to one side of the square until they match. Drive another screw through each slat and into each stringer. Cut some 4½"-wide spacers to set the gaps between panel slats, and attach the remaining slats to the same side of the stringers with two screws driven at each joint. Make sure the bottoms of the slats stay aligned **(photo D)**. Turn the panel over and attach slats to the other side, starting 4½" from the ends so the slats

are staggered on opposite sides of the stringers—there will only be three slats on this side. Build the long panel the same way.

CONTOUR THE PANEL TOPS. To lay out the curve at the top of each fence panel, you will need to make a marking guide. Cut a thin, flexible strip of wood to a length at least 6" longer than each fence panel. Tack nails at the top outside corner of each end slat, and tack another nail at the center of each panel (from side to side), ½" up from the top stringer. Position the flexible guides so the ends are above the nails at the ends of the panels, and the midpoints are below the nails in the centers of the panels, forming smooth curves in the flexible guides. Trace the contour created by each curve onto the tops of the slats **(photo E).** Cut the contours with a jig saw, using a blade short enough that it will not strike the slats on the other side. Repeat the steps on the other side of each panel—because of the thickness of the fence panels, you will need to mark and cut one side at a time. Sand the cuts smooth.

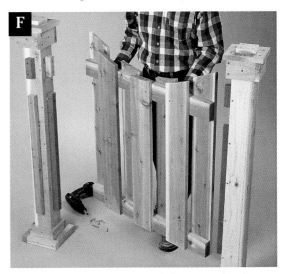
Set the completed fence panels between the cleats on the faces of the posts.

APPLY FINISHING TOUCHES. Position the fence panels between the posts so the top stringer in each panel fits in the gap between the long and short post cleats **(photo F).** Drive screws through the slats and into the cleats to fasten the panels to the posts. We applied exterior wood stain to protect the cedar. Set the trash can corral in your trash area. If need be, you can raise the height of any of the posts slightly by detaching the base collar, lifting the post, and reattaching the collar.

PROJECT
POWER TOOLS

Luminary

*Dress up your yard or garden with these warm, decorative
accents that look even better in bunches.*

CONSTRUCTION MATERIALS

Quantity	Lumber
1	2 × 8 × *" cedar
1	1 × 2" × 8' cedar
1	1"-wide × 5' copper strip

*The shortest length available at most lumber
yards is 6'. Since this is much more than you
need for a single luminary, ask a yardworker if
they have any scraps that are at least 6" long.

Luminaries are decorative
outdoor accents that
hold and protect candles
or glass lamp chimneys. Traditionally, they are arranged in
groups around an entrance or
along a garden pathway. The
simple slat-built luminary design shown here is easy and inexpensive to make. All you
need are a few pieces of 1 × 2

cedar, some 1"-thick strips of
copper and a 6"-dia. cedar
base. The copper trim, glass
chimneys and candles can be
purchased at most craft stores.
We used 22-gauge copper
strips, which are thin enough to
cut with scissors and will form
easily around the luminary.
Make sure to use copper nails
to attach the strips.

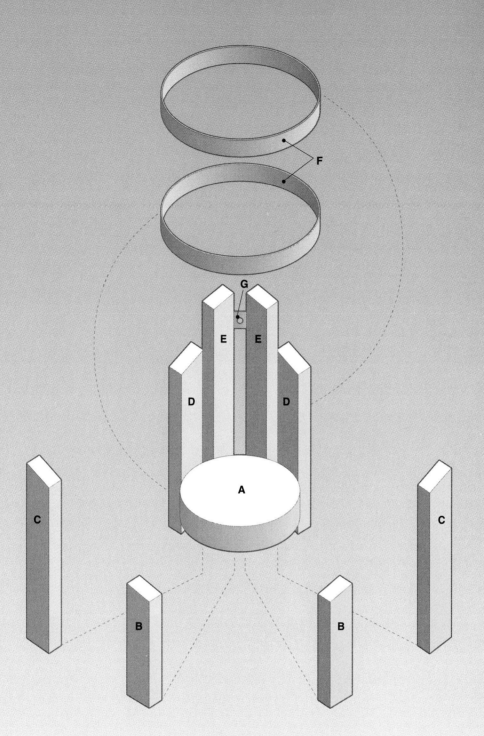

Cutting List

Key	Part	Dimension	Pcs.	Material
A	Base	1½ × 6 × 6"	1	Cedar
B	Front slat	⅞ × 1½ × 8"	2	Cedar
C	Short slat	⅞ × 1½ × 10"	2	Cedar
D	Middle slat	⅞ × 1½ × 12"	2	Cedar

Cutting List

Key	Part	Dimension	Pcs.	Material
E	Back slat	⅞ × 1½ × 14"	2	Cedar
F	Strap	1 × 25"	2	Copper
G	Hanger	1 × 3½"	1	Copper

Materials: 1⅝" deck screws, ¾" copper nails, candle and glass candle chimney.

Note: Measurements reflect the actual size of dimensional lumber.

Directions: Luminary

MAKE THE BASE. The base for the luminary is a round piece of cedar cut with a jig saw. Because the luminary slats are attached to the sides of the base, it is important that the base be as symmetrical and smooth as you can get it. Start by cutting the base (A) to 7¼" in length from a piece of 2 × 8 cedar (this will result in a square workpiece). Draw diagonal lines between opposite corners. The point where the lines intersect is the center of the board. Set the point of a compass at the centerpoint, and draw a 6"-dia., circular cutting line with the compass. Cut the base to shape along the cutting line, using a jig saw with a coarse-wood cutting blade (thicker blades are less likely to "wander" than thinner blades). Clamp a belt sander to your worksurface on its side, making sure the sanding belt is perpendicular to the worksurface. Sand the edges of the base to smooth out any rough spots, using the belt sander as a stationary grinder **(photo A).** If you are making more than one luminary, cut and sand all the bases at once for greater efficiency.

MAKE THE SLATS. The sides of each luminary are formed by four pairs of 1 × 2 cedar, cut to different lengths. All the slats are mitered on their top ends for a decorative effect that moves upward from front to back. Start by cutting the front slats (B), short slats (C), middle slats (D) and back slats (E) to length. On one slat, mark a

TIP

Prevent copper from oxidizing and turning green by coating it with spray-on polyurethane.

Smooth out the edges of the luminary base with a belt sander clamped to your worksurface.

Make a miter cut at the top of one slat, then use that slat as a guide for marking miter cuts on the rest of the slats.

point on one long edge, ½" in from an end. Draw a straight line from the point to the corner at the opposite edge. Cut along the line with a saw and miter box or with a power miter box. Using this slat as a guide, trace mitered cutting lines onto the tops of all the slats **(photo B).** Miter-cut the rest of the slats along the cutting lines.

ATTACH THE SLATS TO THE BASE. To attach the slats to the base, first drill a pair of ⅛"-dia. pilot holes at the bottom of

each slat. The pilot holes should be staggered to avoid splitting the base; drill one pilot hole ½" from the side and 1" up from the bottom; drill the other pilot hole ½" from the other side and 1½" up from the bottom. Countersink the pilot holes enough so the screw heads will be recessed. The slats should be installed so miters form a gradual upward slope from front to back (see *Diagram,* page 53). It is also important that the spacing between slats be exactly the same

Use ⅞"-wide spacers to maintain the gaps between the slats as you attach them to the base.

so that slats on opposite sides of the base are aligned. Use four ¾"-wide spacers to accomplish this. First, set the base on a ½"-thick block to create a recess. Then, arrange the four spacers in a stack so they form a hub over the center of the base (from above, the spacers should look like a pie cut into eight equal-sized pieces). Set the slats between the spacers so the bottoms are resting on the worksurface and they are flush against the base. Adjust the positions of the slats and spacers until each slat is opposite a slat across the base. Once you get the layout set, you may want to wrap a piece of masking tape around the slats, near the bottom, to hold them in place while you fasten them to the base. Now, carefully drive a 1⅝" deck screw through each pilot hole in each slat, and into the base **(photo C).** Do not overtighten the screws. Remove the spacers.

ATTACH THE STRAPS. We wrapped two 1"-wide straps made of 22-gauge (fairly lightweight) copper around the luminary to brace the slats. Try to find copper strips that are 25" long or longer at your local craft store. If you cannot find any strips that are that long, buy the shorter ones and splice them together with a 1" overlapping seam. Cut two 1"-wide copper strips to 25" in length to make the straps (F). Ordinary scissors will cut thin copper easily. Test-fit the straps by taping them in place around the slats. Mark drilling points for guide holes on the copper strap—one hole per slat, centered between the top and bottom of the strap. Drill ¹⁄₁₆"-dia. pilot holes through the drilling points, reposition the straps around the luminary (the bottom strap should conceal the screws heads at the bottoms of the slats). The second strap should be about 6¼" up from the bottom of the luminary. Insert a 6"-long block of wood between two slats that are opposite one another, then drive a ¾" copper nail through the pilot holes in those straps to secure them to the slats **(photo D).** Move the block, and drive copper nails through the rest of the pilot holes.

APPLY FINISHING TOUCHES. If you want to hang your luminary from a wall or post, cut a 1 × 3½"-long strip of copper to make a hanger (G). Drill a ⅜"-dia. hole through the center, then nail the hanger to the outsides of the back slats, about 1" down from the tops. To make a centering pin for holding a candle to the base, drive a 1¾" screw or a 6d nail up through the center of the base. Apply a coat of exterior wood stain if you plan to keep the luminary outdoors.

Brace the slats with a spacer as you tack on the copper strips.

Garden Bridge

Whether it's positioned over a small ravine or a swirl of stones,
this handsome bridge will add romance and charm to your yard.

CONSTRUCTION MATERIALS

Quantity	Lumber
4	4 × 4" × 8' cedar
2	2 × 10" × 8' cedar
10	2 × 4" × 8' cedar
2	1 × 8" × 8' cedar
2	1 × 3" × 8' cedar
8	1 × 2" × 8' cedar
2	½" × 2 × 8' cedar lattice

A bridge can be more than simply a way to get from point A to point B without getting your feet wet. This striking cedar footbridge will be a design centerpiece in any backyard or garden. Even if the nearest trickle of water is miles from your home, this garden bridge will give the impression that your property is graced with a tranquil brook, and you'll spend many pleasurable hours absorbing the peaceful images it inspires. You can fortify the illusion of flowing water by laying a "stream" of landscaping stones beneath this garden bridge. If you happen to have a small ravine or waterway through your yard, this sturdy bridge will take you across it neatly and in high style.

OVERALL SIZE:
46½" HIGH
38½" WIDE
97" LONG

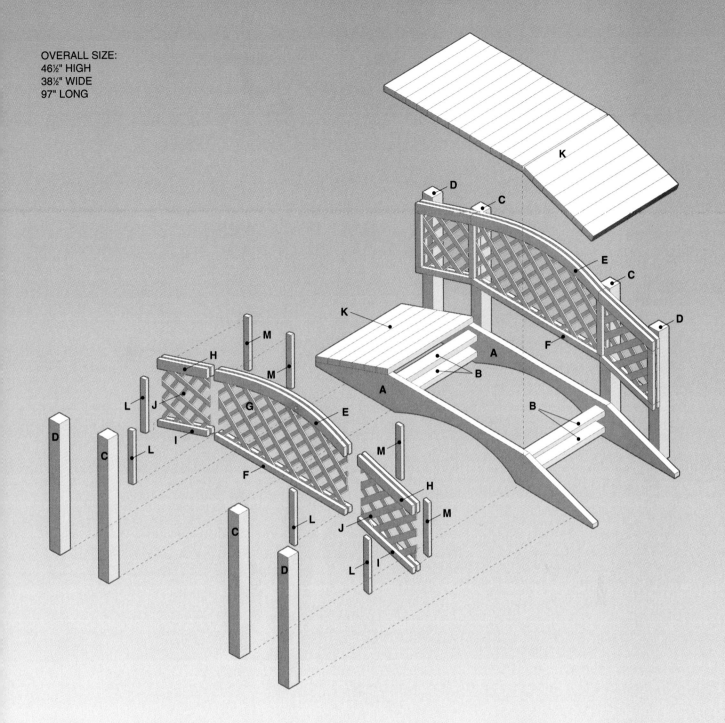

Cutting List				
Key	**Part**	**Dimension**	**Pcs.**	**Material**
A	Stringer	1½ × 9¼ × 96"	2	Cedar
B	Stretcher	1½ × 3½ × 27"	4	Cedar
C	Middle post	3½ × 3½ × 42"	4	Cedar
D	End post	3½ × 3½ × 38"	4	Cedar
E	Center handrail	1½ × 7¼ × 44½"	4	Cedar
F	Center rail	⅞ × 1½ × 44½"	4	Cedar
G	Center panel	½ × 23½ × 44½"	2	Cedar lattice

Cutting List				
Key	**Part**	**Dimension**	**Pcs.**	**Material**
H	End handrail	⅞ × 2¼ × 19½"	8	Cedar
I	End rail	⅞ × 1½ × 24"	8	Cedar
J	End panel	½ × 19 × 24"	4	Cedar lattice
K	Tread	1½ × 3½ × 30"	26	Cedar
L	Filler strip	⅞ × 1½ × 19"	8	Cedar
M	Trim strip	⅞ × 1½ × 21"	8	Cedar

Materials: Lag screws (⅜ × 4"), deck screws (2", 3"), finishing materials.

Note: All measurements reflect the actual size of dimensional lumber.

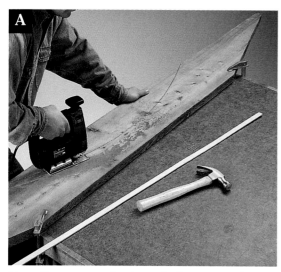

Use a jig saw to make the arched cutouts in the bottoms of the 2 × 10 stringers.

Attach pairs of stretchers between the stringers with 3" deck screws.

Directions: Garden Bridge

MAKE THE STRINGERS. The first step in building the base involves cutting two long, heavy boards, called stringers (A), to shape. The stringers are the main structural members of the bridge. Both stringers have arcs cut into their bottom edges. The ends of the stringers are cut at a slant to create the gradual tread incline of the garden bridge. Start by cutting the stringers (A) to size. Before cutting the stringers to shape, carefully draw several guidelines on the workpieces: first, draw a centerline across the width of each stringer; then mark two more lines across the width of each stringer, 24" to the left and right of the centerline; finally, mark the ends of each stringer, 1" up from one long edge, and draw diagonal lines from these points to the top of each line to the left and right of the center. Use a circular saw to cut the ends of the stringers along the diagonal lines. Next, tack a nail on the centerline, 5¼" up from the same long

Cut the 4 × 4 posts to their finished height, then use lag screws to attach them to the outsides of the stringers.

edge. Also tack nails along the bottom edge, 20½" to the left and right of the centerline. To lay out the arc at the bottom of each stringer, you will need to make a marking guide from a thin, flexible strip of scrap wood or plastic. Hook the middle of the marking guide over the center nail and slide the ends under the outside

nails to form a smooth curve. Trace along the guide with a pencil to make the cutting line for the arc (you can mark both stringers this way, or mark and cut one, then use it as a template for marking the other). Remove the nails and marking guide, and cut the arcs on the bottom edge of each stringer with a jig saw **(photo A).**

Attach the treads to the stringers with deck screws.

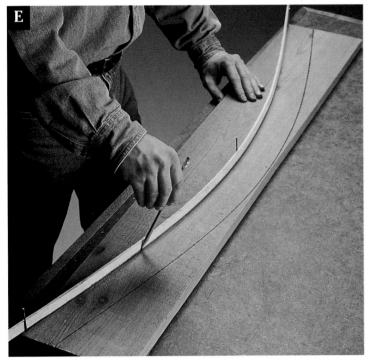

Use a flexible piece of plastic or wood as a marking guide when drawing the cutting lines for the center handrails.

ASSEMBLE THE BASE. Once the two stringers are cut to shape, they are connected with four straight boards, called stretchers (B), to form the base of the bridge. Posts that support the handrails are then attached to the base. These posts will also support the decorative lattice panel frames. Cut the stretchers (B), middle posts (C) and end posts (D) to size. Mark the stretcher locations on the insides of the stringers, 1½" from the top and bottom of the stringers. The outside edges of the stretchers should be 24" from the centers of the stringers (see *Diagram*, page 57), leaving the inside edges flush with the bottoms of the arcs. Stand the stringers upright and position the stretchers between them. Support the bottom stretchers with 1½"-thick spacer blocks for correct spacing. Fasten the stretchers between the stringers with countersunk 3" deck screws, driven through the stringers and into the ends of the stretchers. Turn the stringer assembly upside down, and attach the top stretchers **(photo B).** The footbridge will get quite heavy at this stage: you may want to build the rest of the project on-site. Clamp the middle posts to the outsides of the stringers so their outside edges are 24" from the center of the stringers. Make sure the middle posts are perpendicular to the stringers. Drill ¼"-dia. pilot holes through the stringers and into the middle posts. Attach the middle posts with ⅜"-dia. × 4"-long lag screws, driven through the stringers and into the posts **(photo C).** Clamp the end posts to the stringers, starting 7" from the stringer ends. Drill pilot holes and secure the end posts to the stringers with lag screws.

ATTACH THE TREADS. Cut the treads (K) to size. Position the treads on the stringers, making sure to space them evenly. The treads should be separated by gaps of about ¼". Test-fit all the treads before you begin installing them. Then, secure the treads with 3"-long countersunk deck screws **(photo D).**

> TIP
>
> *Lattice panels need to be handled carefully, or they may fall apart. This is especially true when you are cutting the lattice panels. Before making any cuts, clamp two boards around the panel, close to the cutting line, to stabilize the lattice and protect it from the vibration of the saw. Always use a long, fine blade on your saw when cutting lattice.*

Use a jig saw to cut the panels and center handrails to shape.

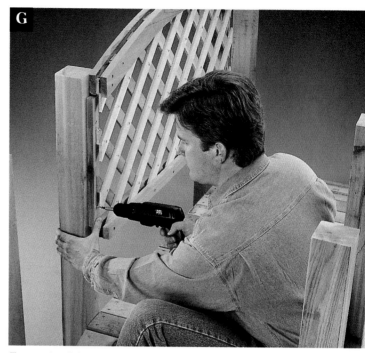

Fasten 1 × 2 filler strips to the posts to close the gaps at the sides of the lattice panels.

ATTACH THE CENTER HAND-RAIL PANELS. The center panels are made by sandwiching lattice sections between 1 × 2 cedar frames. Each center panel has an arc along its top edge. This arc can be laid out with a flexible marking guide, using the same procedures used for the stringers. Once the center panels are made, they are attached to the inside faces of the middle posts. Start by cutting the center handrails (E), center rails (F) and center panels (G) to size. Using a flexible marking guide, trace an arc that begins 2½" up from one long edge of one center handrail. The top of this arc should touch the top edge of the workpiece. Lower the flexible marking guide 2½" down on the center handrails. Trace this lower arc, starting at the corners, to mark the finished center handrail shape **(photo E).** Using a jig saw, cut along the bottom arc. Trace the fin-ished center handrail shapes onto the other workpieces, and cut along the bottom arc lines. Cut the center panels (G) to size from ½"-thick cedar lattice. Sandwich each center panel between a pair of center handrails so the top and side edges are flush. Clamp the parts, and gang-cut through the panel and center handrails along the top arc line with a jig saw **(photo F).** Unfasten the boards, and sand the curves smooth. Refasten the center panels between the arcs, ½" down from the tops of the arcs. Drive 2" deck screws through the inside center handrail and into the center panel and out-side center handrail. Drive one screw every 4 to 6"—be sure to use pilot holes and make an effort to drive screws through areas where the lattice strips cross, so the screws won't be visible from above. Fasten the center rails to the bottom of the center panels, flush with the bottom edges. Center the pan-els between the middle posts, and fasten them to the posts so the tops of the handrails are flush with the inside corner of the middle posts at each end. The ends of the handrails are positioned at the center of the posts. Drive 3" deck screws through the center handrails and center rails to secure the panel to the center posts. Cut the filler strips (L) to size. The filler strips fit between the cen-ter handrails and center rails, bracing the panel and provid-ing solid support for the loose ends of the lattice. Position the filler strips in the gaps between the center panels and the middle posts, and fasten them to the middle posts with 2" deck screws **(photo G).**

ATTACH THE END HANDRAIL PANELS. Like the center panels, the end panels are made by sandwiching cedar lattice sec-tions between board frames and fastening them to posts.

Clamp the rough end panels to the posts at the ends of the bridge, and draw alignment markers so you can trim them to fit exactly.

The ends of the end panels and the joints between the end and center panels are covered by trim strips (M), which are attached with deck screws. This is the final step in building the garden bridge. Cut the end handrails (H), end rails (I) and end panels (J) to size. Position an end handrail and an end rail on your worksurface. Position an end panel over the pieces. Adjust the end handrail and end rail so the top of the panel is ½" down from the top edge of the end handrail. Sandwich the end panels between another set of end handrails and end rails, and attach the parts with 2" deck screws. Then clamp or hold the panels against the end posts and middle posts. Adjust the end panels so they are aligned with the center panel and the top inside corner of the end post. To cut the end panels to size, draw alignment marks near the end of the panel along the outside of the end post **(photo H).** Unclamp the panels, and draw cutting lines connecting the alignment marks. Cut along the lines with a jig saw. Sand the end panels, and attach them to the posts with countersunk 3" deck screws, driven through the end handrails and end rails. Slide filler strips between the end panels and the posts. Fasten the filler strips with 2" deck screws. Cut the trim strips (M) to size. Attach the trim strips over each joint between the end and center panels, and at the outside end of each end panel, with countersunk 3" deck screws **(photo I).**

APPLY FINISHING TOUCHES. Sand all the surfaces to smooth out any rough spots, and apply an exterior wood stain to protect the wood, if desired. You may want to consider leaving the cedar untreated, since that will cause the wood to turn gray—this aging effect may help the bridge blend better with other yard elements. Get some help, and position the bridge in your yard. For a dramatic effect, dig a narrow, meandering trench between two distinct points in your yard, line the trench with landscape fabric, then fill the trench with landscaping stones to simulate a brook.

Use deck screws to attach a trim strip over each joint between the end panels and center panels.

Fold-up Lawn Seat

*With this fold-up seat built for two, you don't have to
sacrifice comfort and style for portability.*

CONSTRUCTION MATERIALS

Quantity	Lumber
1	2 × 8" × 6' cedar
4	2 × 4" × 8' cedar
2	1 × 6" × 8' cedar

Even though this cedar
lawn seat folds up for
easy transport and stor-
age, it is sturdier and more attractive than just about any
outdoor seating you are likely
to make or buy. The backrest
and legs lock into place when
the seat is in use. To move or
store this two-person seat, simply fold the backrest down and
tuck the legs into the seat

frame to convert the seat into a
compact package.

Because it is portable and
stores in a small space, you can
keep the fold-up lawn seat
tucked away in a garage or
basement and set it up for extra
seating when you are entertain-
ing. Or, if security around your
home is an issue, you can bring
it inside easily during times
when you're not home.

OVERALL SIZE:
34⅛" HIGH
20" DEEP
42" LONG

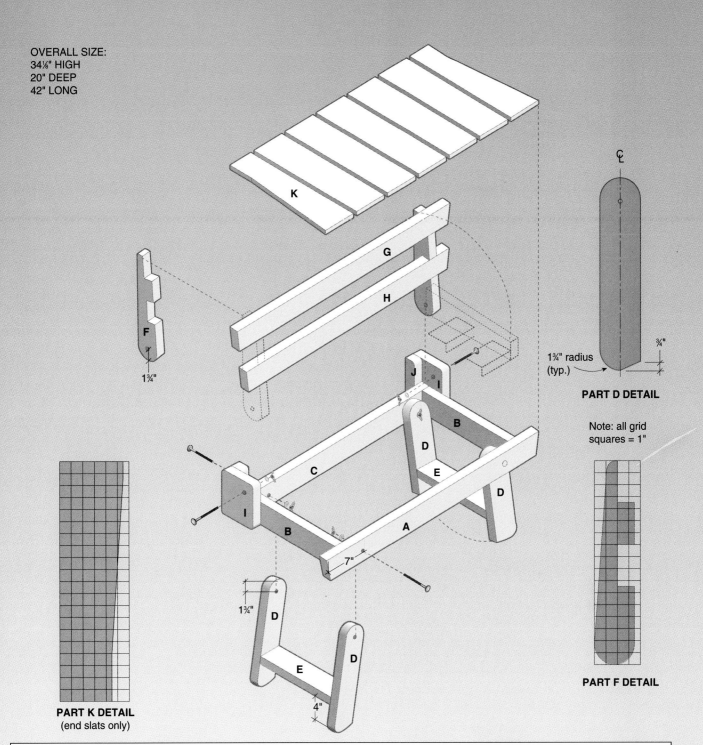

PART D DETAIL

1¾" radius
(typ.)

¾"

Note: all grid
squares = 1"

PART F DETAIL

PART K DETAIL
(end slats only)

7"

1¾"

4"

Cutting List				
Key	Part	Dimension	Pcs.	Material
A	Front seat rail	1½ × 3½ × 42"	1	Cedar
B	Side seat rail	1½ × 3½ × 17"	2	Cedar
C	Back seat rail	1½ × 3½ × 35½"	1	Cedar
D	Leg	1½ × 3½ × 16¼"	4	Cedar
E	Stretcher	1½ × 3½ × 13⅞"	2	Cedar
F	Backrest post	1½ × 3½ × 17"	2	Cedar

Cutting List				
Key	Part	Dimension	Pcs.	Material
G	Top rest	1½ × 3½ × 42"	1	Cedar
H	Bottom rest	1½ × 3½ × 40"	1	Cedar
I	Cleat	1½ × 6 × 7¼"	2	Cedar
J	Stop	1½ × 2 × 7¼"	2	Cedar
K	Slat	⅞ × 5½ × 20"	7	Cedar

Materials: Moisture-resistant glue, ⅜ × 4" carriage bolts (6) with washers and wing nuts, deck screws (1¼", 2", 2½").

Note: Measurements reflect the actual size of dimensional lumber.

Directions:
Fold-up Lawn Seat

MAKE THE LEGS. The lawn seat is supported by two H-shaped legs that fold up inside the seat. Start by cutting the legs (D) to the length shown in the *Cutting List* on page 63. Mark a point 1¾" in from one end of each leg, centered side to side. Set the point of a compass at each point and draw a 1¾"-radius semicircle to make cutting lines for roundovers at the ends of the legs (these ends will be the tops of the legs). Then, drill a ⅜"-dia. guide hole through each point. At the other end of each leg, mark a centerpoint measured from side to side. Measure in ¾" from the end along one edge, and mark another point. Connect the points with a straight line, and cut along the line with a jig saw to create the flat leg bottoms that will contact the ground. Then mark 1¾"-radius roundovers at the opposite edges of the leg bottoms. Cut the roundovers with a jig saw. Attach a stretcher (E) between each pair of legs so the bottoms of the stretchers are 4" up from the bottoms of the legs **(photo A).** Use moisture-resistant wood glue and 2½" deck screws driven through countersunk pilot holes to attach the stretchers, making sure the flat ends of the legs are on the same side of the stretcher.

MAKE THE BACKREST POSTS. Two posts are notched to hold the two boards that form the backrest. Cut the backrest posts (F) to size. On one edge of each post, mark points 6½", 10" and 13½" up from the end of the post. Draw a line lengthwise on each post, 1½" in from the edge with the marks. Extend lines out from each point so they cross the lengthwise line. This will create the outlines for cutting notches in the post (see *Diagram,* page 63). Use a jig saw to cut out the notches, then file or sand the cuts smooth **(photo B).** Use a compass to draw a semicircle with a 1¾" radius at the bottom of each post. Measure up 1¾" from the bottoms, and mark drilling points that are centered side to side. Drill a ⅜"-dia. guide hole through each drilling point to complete the posts. Using the *Part F Detail* as a guide, mark the 1" tapers on the back edges of the posts, as well as the 1¾"-radius roundovers at the bottoms of the posts. Make these cuts with a jig saw, then sand the posts smooth. Sand a little extra off the top to dull any sharp edges.

ASSEMBLE THE BACKREST. Cut the top rest (G) and bottom rest (H). Mark trim lines at both ends of each board, starting ½" in from the ends on one edge and tapering to the opposite corner. Trim off the ends along these lines with a jig saw. Position the posts on their back (tapered) edges, and insert the top and bottom rests into their notches. Position the posts 32½" apart. Center the rests on the posts so the overhang is equal on each rest, and attach the rests to the posts with glue and 2" deck screws **(photo C).**

BUILD THE SEAT FRAME. The seat frame is made by attaching two posts between a front rail and back rail. The front rail is tapered to match the backrest. Start by cutting the front seat rail (A), side seat rails (B) and back seat rail (C) to length. Sand the parts to smooth out any rough edges. Drill a pair of evenly spaced, countersunk pilot holes for 2½" deck screws, 4" in from each end of the front rail to attach the posts, then drill centered, ⅜"-dia. holes, 7" in from each end for the leg assemblies. Also drill ⅜"-dia. pilot holes for carriage bolts through the back rail, centered 3¾" in from each end. Make a ½" taper cut at each end of the front rail. Apply moisture-resistant glue to one end of each post, and position the side rails against the front rails. Fasten the side rails to the back of the front rail by driving deck screws through the pilot holes and into the ends of the side rails. Fasten the back rail to the free ends of the side rails with glue and screws. Make sure the ends are

Fasten the stretchers between the legs with glue and deck screws.

Smooth out the post notches with a wood file.

Center the top and bottom rests in the post notches, and fasten them with glue and deck screws.

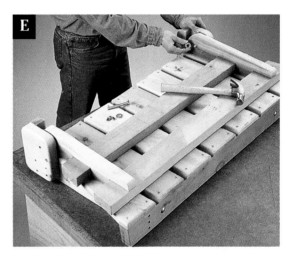

Attach the cleats and stops to the rear edges of the seat frame.

flush. Sand the frame to round over the bottom, outside edges.

JOIN THE LEGS & SEAT FRAME. Position the leg assemblies inside the seat frames, making sure the rounded corners face the ends of the frame. Apply paste wax to four carriage bolts. Align the guide holes in the legs and seat frame, then attach the parts with the carriage bolts (see *Diagram*).

ATTACH THE CLEATS & STOP. The cleats (I) and stops (J) are attached to each other on the back corner of the seat frame to provide an anchor for the backrest. Once the cleats and stops are attached, carriage bolts are driven through the cleats and into the posts on the backrest. Cut the cleats and stops to size. The stops fit flush against the back edges of the cleats. As its name suggests, the stop supports the backrest and prevents it from folding all the way over when you sit on the chair. Position a stop against a cleat face, flush with one long edge. Make sure the top and bottom edges are flush, and attach the stop to the cleat with glue and 2" deck screws. Drill a

⅜"-dia. hole through each cleat, centered 1¾" in from the front and top edges. Smooth the edges of the cleats and stops with a sander, and attach them to the rear corners of the seat frame with glue and deck screws **(photo D).** Make sure the bottom edges of the cleats and stops are ½" up from the bottom of the frame.

ATTACH THE SEAT SLATS. The seat slats are all the same length, but the end slats are tapered from front to back. Cut the slats (K), then plot out a 1"-grid pattern onto two of the slats. Use the *Part K Detail* as a guide for drawing cutting lines at the edges of the two slats (note that the taper straightens out 4" from the back of the slat). Cut the tapers with a circular saw or jig saw. Smooth out all the edges of all the seat slats with a router and roundover bit, or with a sander, then attach the slats to the seat frame. Make sure the wide ends of the end slats are flush with the ends of the frame, and the back ends of all slats are flush with the back edge of the frame. The gaps between slats

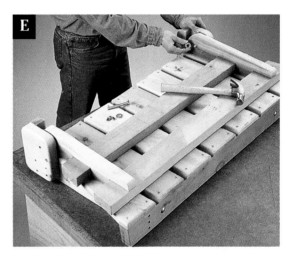

Attach the backrest to the seat frame with carriage bolts and wing nuts.

should be equal. Use glue and 2" screws to secure the slats.

ASSEMBLE THE LAWN SEAT. Finish all the parts with an exterior wood stain. Fit the backrest assembly between the cleats. Align the carriage bolt holes in the posts and cleats, and insert the bolts. Add washers and wing nuts to the free ends to secure the backrest to the seat frame **(photo E).** Hand-tighten the wing nuts to lock the backrest and legs in position. Loosen the wing nuts when you want to fold up the lawn seat for transport or storage.

Gardener's Tote

*Organize and transport your essential gardening supplies
with this handy cedar tote box.*

Quantity	Lumber
1	1 × 10" × 6' cedar
1	1 × 6" × 6' cedar
1	1 × 4" × 6' cedar
1	1 × 2" × 6' cedar

This compact carrying tote has plenty of room and is a real blessing for gardeners. With special compartments sized for seed packages, spray cans and hand tools, it is a quick and easy way to keep all your most-needed supplies organized and ready to go. The bottom shelf is well suited for storing kneeling pads or towels. The gentle curves cut into the sides of the storage compartment make access easy and provide a nice decorative touch. The sturdy cedar handle has a comfortable hand-grip cutout. You'll find this tote to be an indispensible gardening companion, whether you're tending a small flower patch or a sprawling vegetable garden.

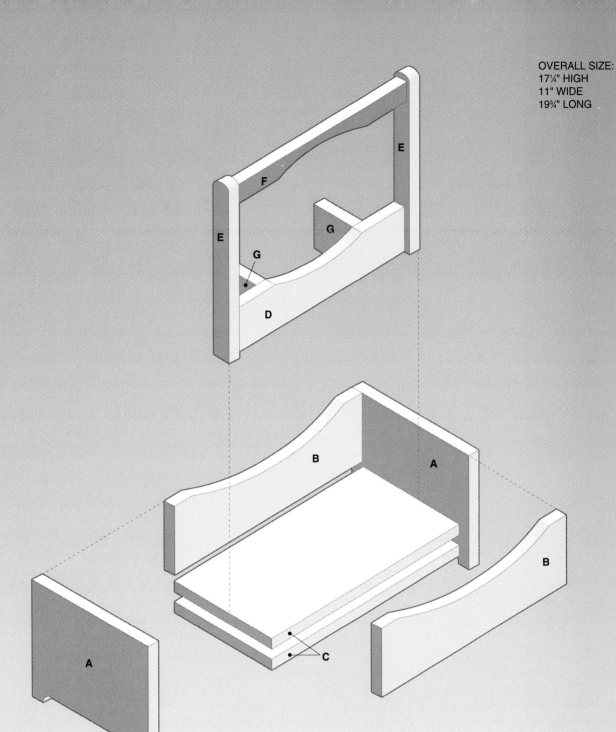

OVERALL SIZE:
17¼" HIGH
11" WIDE
19¾" LONG

Cutting List

Key	Part	Dimension	Pcs.	Material
A	End	⅞ × 9¼ × 11"	2	Cedar
B	Side	⅞ × 5½ × 18"	2	Cedar
C	Shelf	⅞ × 9¼ × 18"	2	Cedar
D	Divider	⅞ × 3½ × 16½"	1	Cedar

Cutting List

Key	Part	Dimension	Pcs.	Material
E	Post	⅞ × 1½ × 14"	2	Cedar
F	Handle	⅞ × 3½ × 16¼"	1	Cedar
G	Partition	⅞ × 3½ × 3⅞"	2	Cedar

Materials: Moisture-resistant glue, 2" deck screws, finishing materials.

Note: Measurements reflect the actual size of dimensional lumber.

Use a jig saw to cut the curves on the bottom edge of each end, forming feet for the box.

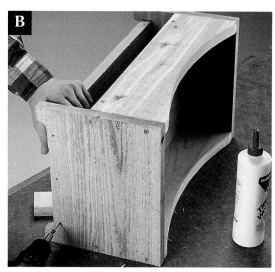

Attach the shelves by driving deck screws through the ends and into the shelf ends.

Directions: Gardener's Tote

BUILD THE BOX. The gardener's tote is essentially a wooden box with a handle and a storage shelf beneath the bottom of the box. The sides of the box have curved cutouts to improve access, and the ends have scalloped cutouts to create feet, making the tote more stable. Start by cutting the ends (A), sides (B) and shelves (C) to size. Sand all parts with medium-grit sandpaper to smooth out any rough edges after cutting. On one side, mark points on one long edge, ½" in from the ends. Mark another point, ½" down from the center of the same long edge. Draw a graceful curve connecting those points, forming the cutting line for the curve at the top. Cut the curve with a jig saw, and sand it to remove any rough spots. Position this completed side piece on the uncut side piece, so their edges and ends are flush. Trace the curve onto the uncut side, and cut that side piece to match the

first. Clamp the sides together, and gang-sand both curves to smooth out any rough spots. To cut the curves on the bottom edges of the ends, first use a compass to draw ¾"-radius semicircles, 1" from each end. These semicircles form the rounded end of each scalloped cutout. Using a straightedge, draw a straight line connecting the tops of the circles, completing the cutout shape. Cut the curves with a jig saw **(photo A),** and sand the ends to remove any saw marks or other rough spots. To attach the ends to the sides, drill pilot holes for countersunk 2" deck screws at each end, ⁷⁄₁₆" in from the edges. Position the pilot holes 1", 3" and 5" down from the tops of the ends. Apply glue to the ends of the sides, and fasten them to the ends with deck screws, driven through the ends and into the sides. Make sure the top and outside edges are flush. Mark the shelf locations on the inside faces of the ends; the bottom of the lower shelf is ¾" up from the bottoms of the ends, and the upper shelf position is 3¾" up from the

bottoms of the ends. Drill pilot holes for 2" deck screws ⁷⁄₁₆" up from the lines. Apply glue to the shelf ends, and position them between the ends with their bottom edges on the lines. Drive 2" deck screws through the ends and into the shelves **(photo B)** to attach the parts.

BUILD THE DIVIDER ASSEMBLY. The internal sections of the gardener's tote are made as a separate assembly and then inserted into the box. Start by cutting the divider (D), posts (E), handle (F) and partitions (G) to size. Use a sander or a jig saw to make a ⅜" roundover on the corners of one end of each post. The divider and handle have shallow arcs cut on one long edge. Draw the arcs on the handle and divider. First, mark points 4" in from each end; then, mark a centered point, ⅝" up from one long edge on the handle. On the divider, mark a centered point ⅝" down from one long edge. Draw a graceful curve to connect the points, and cut along the cutting lines with a jig saw.

Drill countersunk pilot holes through the posts before you attach them to the handle.

TIP

In many cases, seeds, soil additives, and other common gardening supplies should not be stored outdoors in subfreezing weather. If you live in a colder climate, load up your tote with these items in the fall, and store the tote in a warm spot throughout the winter.

Sand all the edges of the handle and divider. Drill two countersunk pilot holes on the divider to attach the partitions. Center the pilot holes ⁷⁄₁₆" to each side of the curve. Use moisture-resistant glue and deck screws, driven through the divider and into the partition edges, to attach the partitions to the divider. Clamp the posts together with their ends flush, and mark a 3½"-long reference line on each post, ⅞" in from the joint formed when the parts are clamped together—start the reference lines at the straight post ends. Connect the lines at the tops to indicate the position of the divider ends. Drill two countersunk pilot holes through the posts, centered between each reference line and the inside edge **(photo C).** Next, drill two countersunk pilot holes in each post, centered ½" and 1" down from the top ends. Position the divider between the posts, aligned with the pilot holes. One face of the divider should be flush with a post edge. Fasten the handle and divider between the posts with moisture-resistant glue

and 2" deck screws. Set the assembly into the box to make sure it fits.

INSTALL THE DIVIDER. Make sure the partitions fit squarely against the sides. Trace post position lines on the ends **(photo D).** Apply glue to the ends where the posts will be fastened. Attach the posts to the ends with countersunk deck screws, driven through

the posts and into the ends. Drive two evenly spaced countersunk screws through the sides and into each outside partition edge.

APPLY THE FINISHING TOUCHES. Sand all the surfaces with medium (100- or 120-grit) sandpaper to smooth out any rough spots, then finish-sand with fine (150- or 180-grit) sandpaper. If you want to preserve the cedar tones, apply exterior wood stain to all the surfaces of the gardener's tote. But you may prefer to simply leave the wood uncoated for a more rustic appearance: as you use the tote, it will slowly turn gray.

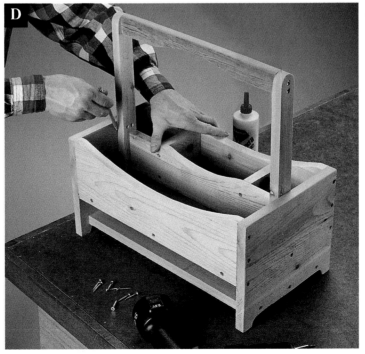

Draw reference lines for the post position on the box ends.

Plant Boxes

Build these simple plant boxes in whichever size or amount best meets your needs.

CONSTRUCTION MATERIALS*

Quantity	Lumber
3	1 × 2" × 8' cedar
6	1 × 4" × 8' cedar
2	⅝" × 4 × 8' fir siding
1	¾" × 4 × 8' CDX plywood

*To build all three plant boxes as shown

Planters and plant boxes come in a vast array of sizes and styles, and there is a good reason for that: everyone's needs are different. So rather than build just one planter that may or may not work for you, we've come up with a planter design that is easy to change to fit your space and planting demands.

We've included measurements for building this plant box in three sizes and shapes: short and broad for flowers or container plants; medium for spices and herbs or small trees and shrubs; and tall and narrow for vegetables or flowering vines that will cascade over the cedar surfaces. The three boxes are proportional to one another, so you can build all three and arrange them in a variety of patterns, including the tiered effect shown above.

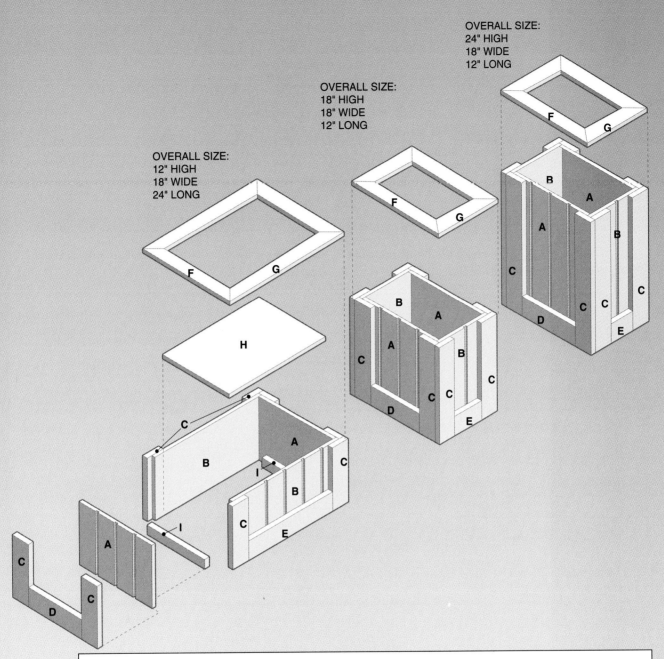

OVERALL SIZE:
24" HIGH
18" WIDE
12" LONG

OVERALL SIZE:
18" HIGH
18" WIDE
12" LONG

OVERALL SIZE:
12" HIGH
18" WIDE
24" LONG

Cutting List								
Key	**Part**	**Front Bin Dimension**	**Pcs.**	**Middle Bin Dimension**	**Pcs.**	**Back Bin Dimension**	**Pcs.**	**Material**
A	End panel	⅝ × 11⅛ × 16¼	2	⅝ × 17⅛ × 16¼	2	⅝ × 23⅛ × 16¼	2	Siding
B	Side panel	⅝ × 11⅛ × 21	2	⅝ × 17⅛ × 9	2	⅝ × 23⅛ × 9	2	Siding
C	Corner trim	⅞ × 3½ × 11⅛	8	⅞ × 3½ × 17⅛	8	⅞ × 3½ × 23⅛	8	Cedar
D	Bottom trim	⅞ × 3½ × 11	2	⅞ × 3½ × 11	2	⅞ × 3½ × 11	2	Cedar
E	Bottom trim	⅞ × 3½ × 15¼	2	⅞ × 3½ × 3¼	2	⅞ × 3½ × 3¼	2	Cedar
F	Top cap	⅞ × 1½ × 18	2	⅞ × 1½ × 18	2	⅞ × 1½ × 18	2	Cedar
G	Top cap	⅞ × 1½ × 24	2	⅞ × 1½ × 12	2	⅞ × 1½ × 12	2	Cedar
H	Bottom panel	¾ × 14 × 18	1	¾ × 14 × 6	1	¾ × 14 × 6	1	Plywood
I	Cleat	⅞ × 1½ × 12	2	⅞ × 1½ × 12	2	⅞ × 1½ × 12	2	Cedar

Materials: Deck screws (1⅝", 3"), 6d galvanized finish nails, and finishing materials.

Note: Measurements reflect the actual thickness of dimensional lumber.

Directions: Plant Boxes

Whatever the size of the plant box or boxes you are building, use the same basic steps for construction. The only difference between the boxes is that the size of some of the components varies from box to box. If you need larger, smaller, broader or taller plant boxes than those shown, it's a fairly easy process to create your own cutting list based on the *Diagram* and dimensions shown on page 71. If you are creating your own dimensions, it is definitely worth your time to double- or triple-check the new part sizes on paper before you actually start to cut the wood. If you are building several planters, do some planning and sketching to make the most efficient use of your wood and to save time by gang-cutting parts that are the same size and shape.

MAKE & ASSEMBLE THE BOX PANELS. The end and side panels are simply rectangular pieces of sheet siding fastened together with galvanized deck screws. We used fir sheet siding with 4"-on-center grooves for a decorative look, but you can substitute any exterior-rated sheet goods (or even dimensional lumber) to match the

Cut the end panels and side panels to size using a circular saw and a straightedge cutting guide.

rest of your yard or home. Start the project by cutting the end panels (A) and side panels (B) to size from ⅝"-thick fir sheet siding using a circular saw and straightedge cutting guide **(photo A).** Lay an end panel face-side-down on a flat work-surface and butt a side panel, face-side-out, up to the end of the end panel. Fasten the side panel to the end panel with 1½" deck screws. Position the second side panel at the other end of the end panel and fasten it with deck screws. Lay the remaining end panel face-side-down on the worksurface. Position the side panel assembly over the end panel, placing the end panel between the side panels and keeping the edges of the side panels flush with the edges of the end panel. Fasten the side panels to the end panel with deck screws. Countersink all screws slightly so the heads are below the surface of the wood.

ATTACH THE TRIM. The cedar trim serves not only as a decorative element, but also as a structural reinforcement to the side panels. Begin the trim in-

stallation by cutting the corner trim (C) to length from 1 × 4 cedar (most cedar has a rough texture on one side; we chose to install our trim pieces with the rough side facing out for a more rustic look, but if you want a more finished appearance, install the pieces with the smooth side facing out). Overlap the edges of the corner trim pieces at the corners to create a square butt joint. Fasten the corner trim pieces directly to the panels with deck screws driven through the inside faces of the panels and into the corner trim pieces **(photo B).** For additional support, drive screws or galvanized finish nails through the overlapping corner trim pieces and into the edges of the adjacent trim piece (this is called "lock-nailing"). Next, cut the bottom trim pieces (D, E) to length from 1 × 4 cedar and fasten the pieces to the end and side panels, between the corner trim pieces. Use 1⅝" deck screws driven through the side and end panels and into the bottom trim pieces.

TIP

Make plant boxes portable by adding wheels or casters. If your yard or garden is partially shaded, attaching locking casters to the base of the plant boxes lets you move your plants to follow the sun, and can even be used to bring the plants indoors during colder weather. Use locking wheels or casters with brass or plastic housings.

Fasten the corner trim to the panels by driving deck screws through the panels into the trim.

INSTALL THE TOP CAPS. The top caps fit around the top of the plant box to create a thin ledge that keeps water from seeping into the end grain of the panels and trim pieces (with the mitered corners, the top caps also add a nice decorative touch). Cut the top caps (F, G) to length from 1 × 2 cedar. Cut 45° miters at both ends of one cap piece, using a power miter saw or a miter box and backsaw. Tack the mitered cap piece to the top edge of the planter, keeping the outside edges flush with the outer edges of the corner trim pieces. To be assured of a proper fit, use this cap piece as a guide for marking and cutting the miters on the rest of the cap pieces. Miter both ends of each piece, then tack it to the box so it makes a square corner with the previously installed piece. If the corners do not work out exactly right, you can loosen the pieces and adjust the arrangement until everything is as square as it can get. Then permanently fasten all the cap pieces to the box with 6d galvanized finish nails.

INSTALL THE BOX BOTTOM. The bottom of the planter box is supported by 1 × 2 cleats (I) that are fastened inside the box, flush with the bottoms of the side and end panels. Cut the cleats to size and screw them to the end panels with 2" deck screws **(photo C).** On the taller bins you may want to mount the cleats higher on the panels so the box won't need as much soil when filled, but if you choose to do this, add cleats on the side panels for ex-

tra support. Cut the bottom panel (H) to size from ¾"-thick exterior-rated plywood (we used CDX plywood). Set the bottom panel onto the cleats (you do not need to use any fasteners to hold it in place).

APPLY FINISHING TOUCHES. After you've built all the boxes, sand all the edges and surfaces to remove rough spots and splinters. Apply two or three coats of exterior wood stain to all the surfaces to protect the wood. When the finish has dried, fill the boxes with potting soil. Or, if you are using shorter boxes, you may prefer to simply place potted plants inside the planter box.

Attach 1 × 2 cleats to the inside faces of the box ends to support the bottom panel.

Compost Bin

*Convert yard waste to garden fertilizer inside this
simple and stylish cedar compost bin.*

CONSTRUCTION MATERIALS

Quantity	Lumber
4	4 × 4" × 4' cedar post
5	2 × 2" × 8' cedar
8	1 × 6" × 8' cedar fence boards

Composting yard debris is an increasingly popular practice that makes good environmental sense. Composting is the process of converting organic waste into rich fertilizer for the soil, usually in a compost bin. A well-designed compost bin has a few key features: it's big enough to contain the organic material

as it decomposes; it allows cross-flow of air to speed along the process; and the bin area is easy to access for adding waste, turning the decomposing compost, and removing the fully composted material. This compost bin has all these features, plus one additional benefit not shared by most compost bins: it is very attractive.

OVERALL SIZE:
30" HIGH
40½" WIDE
48" LONG

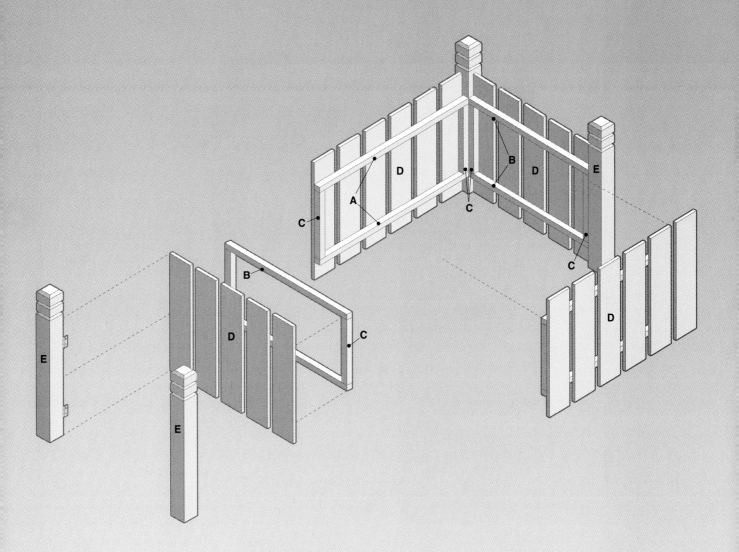

Cutting List

Key	Part	Dimension	Pcs.	Material
A	End rail	1½ × 1½ × 41"	4	Cedar
B	Side rail	1½ × 1½ × 33½"	4	Cedar
C	Cleat	1½ × 1½ × 15"	8	Cedar
D	Slat	¾ × 5½ × 27"	22	Cedar
E	Post	3½ × 3½ × 30"	4	Cedar

Materials: Galvanized deck screws (2" and 3"), hook-and-eye latch mechanism, 3 × 3" brass butt hinges (one pair) and screws.

Note: Measurements reflect the actual thickness of dimensional lumber.

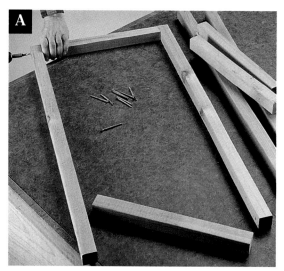

Fasten the cleats between the rails to construct the panel frames.

Attach a slat at each end of the panel frame so the outer edges of the slats are flush with the outer edges of the frame.

Directions: Compost Bin

BUILD THE PANEL FRAMES. The four fence-type panels that make up the sides of this compost bin are simply cedar slats that are attached to panel frames. The panel frames for the front and back of the bin are longer than the frames for the ends of the bin. Cut the end rails (A), side rails (B) and cleats (C) to length from 2 × 2 cedar. Group pairs of matching rails with a pair of cleats. Assemble each group into a frame—the cleats should be between the rails, flush with the ends. Fasten all four panel frames together with 3" deck screws driven through the rails and into each end of each cleat **(photo A)**—drill pilot holes and countersink the screw heads slightly.

ATTACH THE PANEL SLATS. The vertical slats that are attached to the panel frames are cut from 1 × 6 cedar fence boards. They are installed with 1½" spaces between them to allow air to flow into the bin. Cut all of the slats (D). Next, lay the frames on a flat surface and place a slat at each end of each frame. Keep the edges of these outer slats flush with the outside edges of the frame, and let the bottoms of the slats overhang the bottom frame rail by 4". Fasten the outer slats to the frames with 2" deck screws, countersunk slightly **(photo B)**. When the outer slats have been fastened to all of the frames, add slats between each pair of outer slats to fill out the panels.

> **TIP**
>
> *Grass clippings, leaves, weeds and vegetable waste are some of the most commonly composted materials. Just about any formerly living organic material can be composted, but DO NOT add any of the following items to your compost bin:*
> * *animal material or waste*
> * *dairy products other than eggshells*
> * *papers with colored inks*
> *For more information on composting, contact your local library or agricultural extension office.*

Insert a 1½" spacing block between the slats to set the correct gap. Be sure to keep the ends of the slats aligned. Check occasionally with a tape measure to make sure the bottoms of all the slats are 4" below the bottom of the panel frame **(photo C)**.

ATTACH THE FRAMES & POSTS. The four slatted panels are joined with corner posts to make the bin. Three of the panels are attached permanently to the posts, and one of the end panels is installed with hinges and a latch so it can swing open like a gate. You can use plain 4 × 4 cedar posts for the corner posts, or, for a more decorative look, you can buy prefabricated fence posts or deck rail posts with carving or contours at the top ends. For our bin, we used cedar deck rail posts with grooves and rounded corners at the tops. Cut the posts (E) to length. If you are using plain posts, you may want to do some decorative contouring or cutting at the top of each post (or attach post caps). Start the bin-assembly process by standing a post

The inner slats should be 1½" apart, with the ends 4" below the bottom of the frame.

Stand the posts and panels upright, and fasten the panels to the posts by driving screws through the cleats.

upright on a flat worksurface. Set one of the longer slatted panels next to the post, resting on the bottoms of the slats. Hold or clamp the panel to the post, making sure the back of the panel frame is flush with one of the faces of the post. Fasten the panel to the post by driving 3" deck screws through the frame cleats and into the posts—space screws at roughly 8" intervals. Stand another post on end, and fasten the other

end of the panel frame to it, making sure the posts are aligned. Then, fasten one of the shorter panels to the adjoining face of one of the posts—the back faces of the frames should just meet in a properly formed corner **(photo D).** Fasten another post at the free end of the shorter panel; then fasten the other longer panel to the posts so it is opposite the first longer panel. This will create a U-shaped structure.

ATTACH THE GATE. The unattached shorter panel is attached at the open end of the bin with hinges to create a swinging gate for loading and unloading material. If you are planning to apply a finish to your compost bin (you may want to use some exterior wood stain to keep the cedar from turning gray), you'll find it easier to apply the finish before you hang the gate. Set the last panel between the posts at the open end of the bin, and move the sides of the bin slightly, if needed, so there is about ¼" of clearance between each end of the panel and the posts. Remove the gate, then attach a pair of 3" butt hinges to the cleat, making sure the barrels of the hinges extend past the face of the outer slats. Set the panel into the opening, and mark the location of the hinge plates onto the post. Open the hinge so it is flat, and attach it to the post **(photo E).** Attach a hook-and-eye latch to the unhinged end of the panel to hold the gate in a closed position. Make sure all hardware is rated for exterior use.

Attach the hinges to the end panel frame, then fasten to the post.

Birdfeeder Stand

Send an invitation to flocks of colorful backyard guests by hanging birdfeeders from this sturdy cedar stand.

Create a hub of aviary activity in your backyard by building this clever birdfeeder stand. Different species of birds are drawn to different types of food: since this stand can support more than one kind of feeder, you will be able to enjoy the sight of many different species fluttering and roosting in one central area. Because birdfeeders vary widely in size and style, from small and plain to large and fanciful, you can use this stand to focus attention on your favorite feeders, as well as the birds that enjoy them.

One important benefit of this cedar birdfeeder stand is that it has a freestanding, open de-sign, so birds are always in full view as they eat.

The heavy stand base, made from cedar frames, provides ample support for the post and hanging arms. To simplify cleanup of any spilled food (as well as make it accessible to hungry birds), we attached a layer of window screening over the slats in the top of the base. To clean the birdfeeder stand, simply remove the feeders, tip the stand on its side and spray it down with a hose.

CONSTRUCTION MATERIALS

Quantity	Lumber
5	1 × 4" × 8' cedar
3	1 × 6" × 8' cedar
4	2 × 4" × 8' cedar
1	2 × 6" × 6' cedar

OVERALL SIZE:
72" HIGH
35¼" WIDE
35¼" LONG

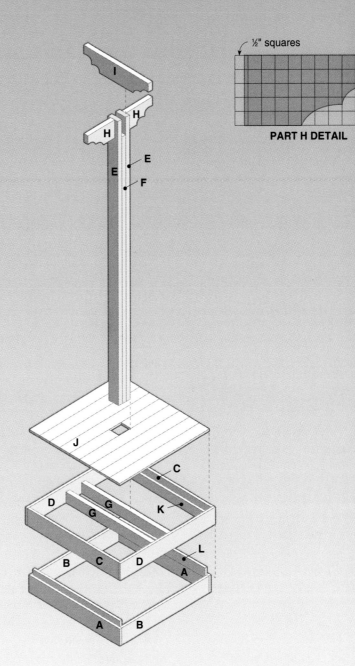

½" squares

PART H DETAIL

Cutting List

Key	Part	Dimension	Pcs.	Material
A	Bottom end	⅞ × 5½ × 33½"	2	Cedar
B	Bottom side	⅞ × 5½ × 32"	2	Cedar
C	Top end	⅞ × 5½ × 33½"	2	Cedar
D	Top side	⅞ × 5½ × 35¼"	2	Cedar
E	Post board	1½ × 3½ × 72"	2	Cedar
F	Post board	1½ × 3½ × 66½"	1	Cedar

Cutting List

Key	Part	Dimension	Pcs.	Material
G	Post support	1½ × 3½ × 31½"	2	Cedar
H	Outside arm	1½ × 5½ × 10¼"	2	Cedar
I	Inside arm	1½ × 5½ × 36"	1	Cedar
J	Floor board	⅞ × 3½ × 33¼"	9	Cedar
K	Floor support	⅞ × 3½ × 31½"	2	Cedar
L	Bottom cleat	⅞ × 3½ × 32"	2	Cedar

Materials: Deck screws (1¼", 2½"), 18 × 36" window screening (2), eye hooks, finishing materials.

Note: Measurements reflect the actual size of dimensional lumber.

Join the top base frame to the bottom base frame by driving screws through the frame cleats.

Use a square to make sure the inside arm is perpendicular to the post before you secure it into the gap at the top of the post.

Directions: Birdfeeder Stand

BUILD THE BASE FRAMES. Two frames are built and then attached, one on top of the other, to form the base. The base gives weight and stability to the birdfeeder stand, while supporting the main post structure. Start by cutting the bottom ends (A), bottom sides (B), top ends (C) and top sides (D) to size. Sand the parts after cutting. Fasten the bottom ends between the bottom sides with deck screws, driven through countersunk pilot holes in the bottom sides. Repeat this procedure with the top sides and top ends to complete the second base frame. Cut the floor supports (K) to size— these parts are attached inside the top frame to form attach-

TIP

There is a real art to making and stocking birdfeeders, identifying species and enjoying bird watching. If you are just a budding ornithologist, make a visit to your local library—the more knowledge you acquire, the more enjoyment you will experience.

ing surfaces for the floorboards that cover the base. Fasten the floor supports to the inside faces of the top ends so the bottoms of the supports are flush with the bottoms of the ends. Cut the bottom cleats (L) to size, and attach them with deck screws to the inside faces of the bottom ends, making sure the top edge of each bottom cleat is 1½" above the top edge of each bottom end. Set the top frame over the bottom frame. Fasten the top and bottom frames together with deck screws, driven through the bottom cleats and into the top frame **(photo A).**

INSTALL POST SUPPORTS. Mark the centerpoints of the top sides on their inside faces. Draw reference lines, 2¼" to each side of the centerpoints. These lines mark the locations for the post supports (G). Cut the post supports to size, and insert them into the top frame so their bottom edges rest on the tops of the bottom sides. Position the post supports so their inside faces are just out-

side the reference lines, then fasten them to the top frame by driving 2½" deck screws through the frame and into the ends of the post supports— countersink the pilot holes slightly so the screw heads are recessed. The completed post structure will be inserted between these supports.

BUILD THE ARMS. Cut the two outside arms (H) and the inside arm (I) to length. Use a pencil to draw a 1"-square grid pattern on one of the arms. Using the grid patterns as a reference (see *Diagram*, page 79), lay out the decorative scallops at the end of the arm. Cut along the layout lines with a jig saw, then use a 1"-dia. drum sander mounted in an electric drill to smooth out the insides of the curves. Use the arm as a template for drawing identical scallops on the other arms. Cut and sand the other arms to match.

MAKE THE POST. The post part of the stand is constructed by sandwiching a middle post board (F) between two side post boards (E). Because the outside arms are attached by screwing through the inside faces of the side post board, it is easier to attach these parts before you assemble the three boards that make up the post. Start by cutting the post boards (E, F). Draw 5½"-long center lines on one face of each side post board, starting at the top. Draw a 5½"-long line, ¾" to each side of the center line, to outline the location for the outside arms on the post. On the center line, drill pilot holes for countersunk deck screws, 1½" and 4½" down from the top edge. Attach the outside arms to the side posts with deck screws, driven through the pilot holes and into the straight ends of the outside arms. Then, sandwich the center post between the side posts so the bottom and side edges are flush. Drive pairs of 2½" deck screws at 8" to 12" intervals, screwing through the face of one side post. Then flip the assembly over and drive screws through the other side post, making sure to stagger them so they do not strike the screws driven from the other side. Center the inside arm in the gap at the top of the post **(photo B).** Secure with 2½" deck screws driven through the side post boards, into the inside arm.

INSTALL THE POST ASSEMBLY. Stand the post up between the post supports in the base frame. Be sure the post is centered between the top frame sides and is perpendicular to the post supports. Drive 2½" deck screws through the post supports and into the post to secure the parts.

MAKE THE FEEDING FLOOR. Floor boards are attached to the floor supports within the

Attach the floor boards by driving deck screws through the floor boards and into the post and floor supports.

top base frame to create a floor. Cut the floor boards (J). One floor board should be cut into two 14½"-long pieces to fit between the post and frame. Arrange the floor boards across the post supports and floor supports, using ¼"-wide scraps to set ¼"-wide gaps between the boards. Fasten the floor boards to the floor supports and post supports with countersunk 1¼" deck screws, driven through the floor boards **(photo C).**

APPLY FINISHING TOUCHES. Apply exterior wood stain to the birdfeeder stand. After it dries, staple two 18 × 36" strips of window screening to the floor to keep food from falling through the gaps **(photo D).** Insert brass screw eyes or other hardware at the ends of the arms to hang your birdfeeders. Set the birdfeeder stand in a semisheltered area in clear view of your favorite window or deck.

Staple window screening over the tops of the floor boards to keep bird food from falling through the gaps.

Tree Surround

*Turn wasted space beneath a mature tree
into a shady seating area.*

Quantity	Lumber
11	2 × 4" × 8' cedar
1	1 × 6" × 10' cedar
20	1 × 4" × 8' cedar

This tree surround with built-in benches provides ample seating in your yard, while protecting the base of the tree trunk. Situated in a naturally shady area, the surround/bench creates an ideal spot to relax with a good book or spend a quiet moment alone.

The tree surround can be built in four pieces in your garage or basement, then assembled on-site to wrap around the tree. As shown, the tree surround will fit a tree trunk up to 30" in diameter. But with some basic math, it's easy to adjust the sizes of the pieces so the surround fits just about any tree in your yard.

Unlike most tree bench designs, this project is essentially freestanding and does not require you to set posts (digging holes at the base of a tree can be next to impossible in some cases). And because it is cedar, it will blend right into most landscapes.

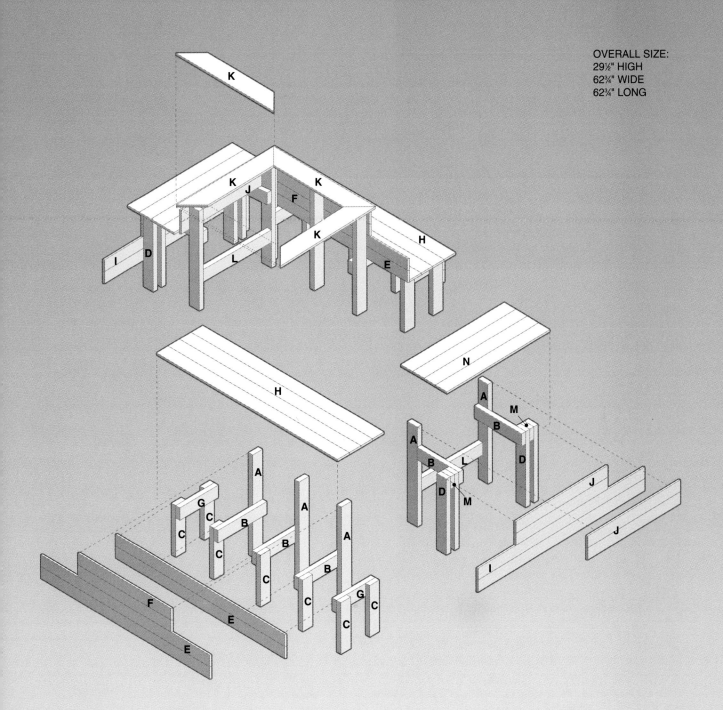

Cutting List

Key	Part	Dimension	Pcs.	Material
A	Inside post	1½ × 3½ × 29½"	10	Cedar
B	Seat rail	1½ × 3½ × 16¾"	10	Cedar
C	Short post	1½ × 3½ × 15"	14	Cedar
D	Long post	1½ × 3½ × 22¼"	8	Cedar
E	Face board	⅞ × 3½ × 60½"	8	Cedar
F	Face board	⅞ × 3½ × 34"	4	Cedar
G	Side seat rail	1½ × 3½ × 13¼"	4	Cedar

Cutting List

Key	Part	Dimension	Pcs.	Material
H	Bench slat	⅞ × 3½ × 62¾"	8	Cedar
I	Face board	⅞ × 3½ × 58¾"	4	Cedar
J	Face board	⅞ × 3½ × 32⅞"	8	Cedar
K	End cap	⅞ × 5½ × 24⅝"	4	Cedar
L	Stringer	1½ × 3½ × 22½"	2	Cedar
M	Nailer	1½ × 3½ × 3½"	4	Cedar
N	Bench slat	⅞ × 3½ × 36⅞"	8	Cedar

Materials: Galvanized deck screws (1½", 2½"), finishing materials.

Note: Measurements reflect the actual size of dimensional lumber.

Directions:
Tree Surround

BUILD THE SHORT BENCH FRAMES. The tree surround is built as two short benches on the sides, and two taller benches on the ends. The benches are joined together to wrap around the tree. To build the support frames for the short benches, cut the inside posts (A), seat rails (B) and short posts (C) to size. Lay a short post on top of an inside post, with the bottom ends flush. Trace a reference line onto the face of the inside post, following the top of the short post. Separate the posts, and lay a seat rail across the faces of the two posts so it is flush with the outside edge and top of the short post, and just below the reference line on the inside post. Use a square to make sure the seat rails are perpendicular to the inside posts and their ends are flush with the post edges, then join the parts with moisture-resistant glue and 2½" deck screws, driven through the seat rails and into the inside posts. Drill a countersunk pilot hole for every screw used in this project. Make six of these assemblies **(photo A).** Cut the four side seat rails (G) to size. Attach them to pairs of short posts so the tops and ends are flush.

ATTACH THE SHORT BENCH FACE BOARDS. The face boards are cut in several different lengths to cover the front of each bench. Cut face boards (E) for the fronts of

Seat rails are attached to the short posts and inside posts to make the bench frames.

The face boards attached at the tops of the short posts on the short benches should extend ⅞" past the edges of the posts.

the short benches to length. Draw lines on the outside faces of these face boards, ⅞" and 14⅛" from each end, and at their centers. These reference lines will serve as guides when you attach the face boards to the short bench frames. Lay two frames made with two

short posts on your worksurface, with the back edges of the back posts flat. Attach a face board to the top edges of the front posts, with 1½" deck screws, so the ends of the face board extend ⅞" beyond the outside edges of the frames (the seat rail should be on the inside of the frame).

Attach face boards to the inside posts to create the backrest. The lowest board should be ⅛" above the seat rails.

TIP

Cover the ground at the base of a tree with a layer of landscaping stone or wood bark before you install a tree surround. To prevent weeds from growing up through the groundcover, lay landscaping fabric in the area first. Add a border of landscape edging to keep everything contained. If the ground at the base of the tree is not level, you can make installation of the tree surround easier by laying a base of landscaping rock, then raking it and tamping it until it is level.

Attach another face board ⅛" below the top face board, making sure the reference lines are aligned **(photo B).**

ASSEMBLE THE SHORT BENCHES. Stand the frame and face board assemblies on their feet, then fit short bench frames made with the inside posts against the inside faces of the face boards. Center the short posts of the frames on the reference lines drawn on the face boards. Attach these frames to the face boards with 2½" deck screws. Then, set another face board at the backs of the seat rails, against the inside posts. Slip a 10d finish nail under the face board where it crosses each seat rail to create a ⅛" gap. Make sure the ends of the face board are flush with the outsides of the end frames, and attach the face board to the inside posts with 1½" deck screws **(photo C).** Attach another face board ⅛" up on the inside posts. Cut face boards (F) to fit across the inside posts with no overhang. Fasten two of these shorter face boards to each bench assembly, so the ends are flush with the outer sides of

the the inside posts. Maintain a ⅛" gap between the face boards. The top edge of the highest face board on each bench assembly should be flush with the tops of the inside posts. Cut the bench slats (H) to size. Center the bench slats on the seat rails, positioning the front bench slat first so it

overhangs the face board by 1⅛" **(photo D).** Attach the front slat by driving two 2½" deck screws through each bench slat and into each seat rail. Attach the rest of the bench slats, making sure the final bench slat on each bench assembly butts against the inside posts.

MAKE THE TALL BENCHES. The two tall benches are built almost exactly like the short benches, except they contain more face boards because of the extra height. They also

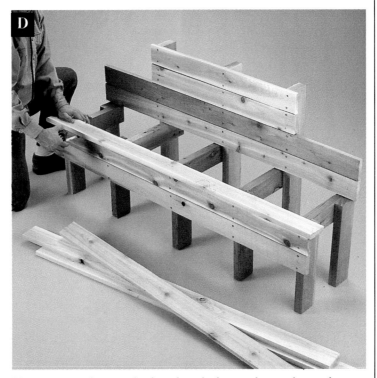

Measure to make sure the front bench slat overhangs the top face board below it by 1⅛".

have doubled posts at the front for extra strength. Cut the long posts (D) and four nailer strips (M). Arrange the long posts in doubled pairs, with nailers in between at the tops. Fasten the doubled posts and nailers together with glue and 2½" deck screws, making sure the nailers are aligned with the fronts and tops of the posts. Then, attach a seat rail to the doubled posts **(photo E).** Attach the free end of each seat rail to an inside post, as you did for the short benches. Cut the stringers (L) to size. Position the stringers between the pairs of inside posts, at the backs of the benches, and attach them by driving deck screws through the inside posts and into the ends of the end stringers. Cut the face boards (I, J) for the tall benches. Use 1½" deck screws to attach two of the shorter boards (J) to the long posts so the top board is flush with the tops of the posts and seat rails, and the ends are flush with the outside edges of the doubled posts **(photo F).** Attach the longer face boards (I) below the shorter face boards, so they overhang the doubled posts by the same amount on each end **(photo G).** The overhang portions will cover the sides of the short benches after assembly. Attach two of the shorter face boards (J) to the front edges of the inside posts, flush with the outside edges. Cut the bench slats (N) for the tall benches. Position the slats on the seat rails, and fasten the front slat so it overhangs the front by 1⅛". Fasten a slat flush against the back of the bench, and fasten the remaining slats on each tall

After making doubled posts for the tall benches, attach the seat rails.

The shorter face boards for the tall benches are attached so the ends are flush with the outsides of the doubled posts.

bench so the spaces between slats are even.

APPLY THE FINISH. Although you are not quite finished cutting parts and you haven't assembled the tree surround yet, now is a good time to apply a finish to the benches. Sand all the surfaces to remove rough spots and splinters, then wipe the wood clean. Apply at least two coats of exterior wood stain to protect the wood.

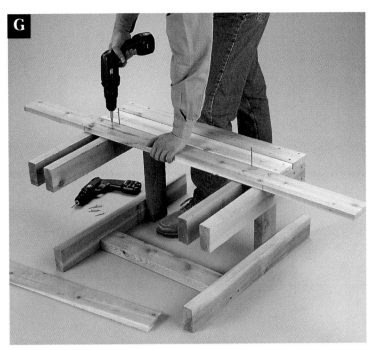

The longer face boards attached to the tall benches overhang the doubled posts so they cover the sides of the short benches when the tree surround is assembled.

ASSEMBLE THE TREE SURROUND. Carry all four benches to the tree you have built the tree surround to fit. Set the benches in a frame around the tree, so the overhang on the tall bench face boards covers the sides of the short benches. The overhanging face boards should fit flush against the recesses created by the slight overhang on the face boards on the short benches. Clamp or tack the benches together. It is likely that you will need to trim the posts on some of the frames to get the tree surround to rest so the bench seats are level. Use a carpenter's level to check the tree surround. If one side is higher than the others, set the level on the bench slats on the higher side, and tip it up until the bubble reads that it is level. Measure the distance from the level to the bench slats, then disassemble the tree

surround and trim that amount from the bottoms of the posts on the higher side. Be very careful in doing this: you are always better off removing less material than you think is necessary, and trimming again if needed. There is no good way to add length to the posts. Once you have trimmed the posts and reassembled the tree surround so it is roughly level, you can make minor adjustments by shimming beneath the posts with flat stones. This leveling process can be a little time-consuming, so be patient as you work.

When the tree surround is level and the benches fit together squarely, attach the tall benches to the short benches by driving 2½" deck screws through face boards on the tall benches and into the posts on the short benches.

ATTACH THE CAP. To give the tree surround a more finished appearance, a 1 × 6 cap with mitered corners is installed over the tops of the inside posts to make a square frame. Cut the caps (K) to full length, then set a cap on the top of one of the benches. Mark the inside corners of the top onto the cap board, then draw 45° miter lines out from the points. Make the miter cuts with a circular saw **(photo H),** or a power miter box if you have one. Attach the cap board to the bench with 1½" deck screws driven through countersunk pilot holes, then cut the three remaining cap pieces to fit, and install them. Apply the same finish to the caps that you applied to the rest of the tree surround.

The 1 × 6 caps are mitered to make a square frame around the top of the tree surround after it is assembled around your tree.

Prairie Windmill

With a mill section that turns and spins in the wind, this lively little windmill becomes the focal point of any garden.

Modeled loosely after the old turn-of-the-century windmills that dotted the prairie landscape, this fun, active garden accent may be just the thing to put some spice into your yard. With a solid, staked base firmly planted on the ground, this windmill spins and turns with the passing breezes.

We used cedar siding for the blades and tail of the mill section. The beveled cedar is the perfect shape and weight for catching the wind, and, because it's cedar, it will withstand the elements. The moving parts spin on lag screws and nylon washers, which perform better with moving parts than metal washers.

Overall, the most impressive part of this prairie windmill may be the geometrically strik-ing tower section, which rises from the base to anchor the spinning mill above. Despite its size, the tower section is very easy to make. You can set the completed windmill in the heart of your garden, or posi-tion it in a corner of your yard to create a unique accent. Either way, you won't be disap-pointed. This is a fun project, and you'll get a glowing sense of satisfaction when you see it spinning and turning in the wind like a real windmill—just the way you built it.

CONSTRUCTION MATERIALS

Quantity	Lumber
2	4 × 4" × 6' cedar
1	2 × 10" × 6' cedar
1	2 × 6" × 6' cedar
1	2 × 4" × 6' cedar
5	2 × 2" × 8' cedar
1	⅝ × 7" × 6' cedar siding
2	¾"-dia. × 3' hardwood dowel

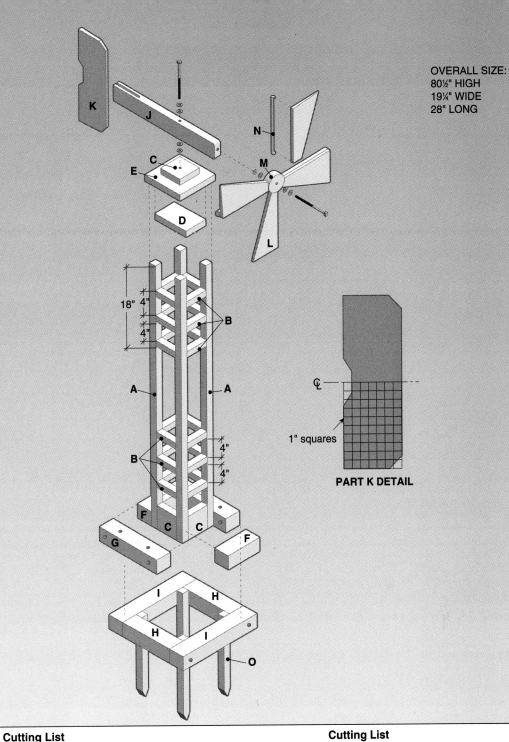

OVERALL SIZE:
80½" HIGH
19¼" WIDE
28" LONG

1" squares

PART K DETAIL

Key	Part	Dimension	Pcs.	Material
A	Post	1½ × 1½ × 60"	4	Cedar
B	Rail	1½ × 1½ × 5"	24	Cedar
C	Spacer	1½ × 5 × 5"	5	Cedar
D	Top insert	1½ × 5 × 8"	1	Cedar
E	Top	1½ × 9¼ × 9¼"	1	Cedar
F	Base end	3½ × 3½ × 8"	2	Cedar
G	Base side	3½ × 3½ × 15"	2	Cedar
H	Foot end	3½ × 3½ × 12"	2	Cedar

Cutting List

Key	Part	Dimension	Pcs.	Material
I	Foot side	3½ × 3½ × 19"	1	Cedar
J	Shaft	1½ × 3½ × 26½"	1	Cedar
K	Tail	⅝ × 7 × 24"	1	Cedar siding
L	Blade	⅝ × 7 × 12"	4	Cedar siding
M	Hub	1½ × 4 × 4"	1	Cedar
N	Backer rod	¾ × ¾ × 13"	4	Dowel
O	Stake	1½ × 1½ × 18"	4	Cedar

Materials: Moisture-resistant glue, epoxy glue, lag screws (³⁄₈ × 6", ³⁄₈ × 8"), deck screws (1¼", 2½", 3"), panhead screws (#4 × 1"), 1"-dia. nylon washers, finishing materials.

Note: Measurements reflect the actual size of dimensional lumber.

Directions:
Prairie Windmill

BUILD THE TOWER FRAME. The main frame for the windmill tower is made up of four posts connected by a series of short rails. Cut the posts (A) and rails (B). Clamp all four posts in a row, and mark the rail locations on all the posts, starting 9" up from one end of the posts and following the spacing shown in the *Diagram* on page 89. Unclamp the posts, and arrange them in pairs. Attach the rails between the posts at the location marks to create two ladderlike assemblies. Use moisture-resistant glue and a single countersunk 2½" deck screw, driven through each post and into each rail. Once the two assemblies are completed, join them together with rails to create the tower frame.

ADD THE TOWER BOTTOM & TOP. Cut the spacers (C), top insert (D), and tower top (E) to size. Four of the spacers are installed between the posts at the bottom of the tower, and the fifth is mounted on top of the tower. Fit four of the spacers between the posts at the bottom, and attach them with glue and 2½" deck screws driven through countersunk pilot holes. On the fifth spacer, draw diagonal lines between opposite corners—the point where the lines intersect is the center of the board. Center the spacer on the tower top (E), and attach it with glue and 1¼" deck screws. Do not drive screws within 1" of the centerpoint. Drill a ¼"-dia. pilot hole for a ⅜"-dia. lag screw through the center, making sure to keep your drill perpendicular—the lag screw is driven later to

secure the windmill to the tower. Next, slip the top insert between the posts at the top of the tower, and fasten the insert with glue and screws. Complete the tower top by centering the spacer and tower top over the top insert and fastening with glue and screws. After assembly is complete, use a power sander to smooth out all sharp edges **(photo A).**

The tower for the windmill is basically two ladder frames joined by rails. Sand sharp edges smooth.

ATTACH THE TOWER BASE. The base of the tower is a heavy frame made from 4 × 4 cedar. When the windmill is installed in your yard, the base is attached to a 4 × 4 frame that is staked into the ground. Cut the base ends (F) and base sides (G) to size. Attach the base ends to the tower with 3" deck screws. To attach the base sides, drill ¼"-dia. pilot holes for ⅜"-dia. lag screws in the base sides, then counterbore the pilot holes with a 1" spade bit. Drive ⅜ × 8" lag screws with metal washers through the base sides and into the base ends. Cut the foot end (H) and foot side (I) to size. Drill pilot holes for counterbored lag screws through the the foot sides, and secure each foot side to the foot ends with a ⅜ × 8" lag screw.

MAKE THE TAIL. Cut the tail (K) to length from beveled cedar lap siding. Draw a 1" grid pattern onto the board, then

draw the shape shown in the *Part K Detail*, page 89. Make sure the notch is on the thick edge. Cut with a jig saw.

MAKE THE SHAFT. Cut the shaft (J) to size from a cedar 2 × 4. Draw a centerline on one long edge of the shaft. Cut a slot into the end of the shaft to hold the tail: first, measure the thickness of the beveled siding at several points, including the thin edge and the thick edge. Using drill bits with the same diameters as the thicknesses of the siding, drill holes along the centerline at points that correspond with the width of the tail—make sure that you drill holes at each end of the slot outline. Connect the holes with a pair of straight lines to create an outline for the tail notch. Cut along the outlines with a handsaw **(photo B).** Next, drill a centered, ⁷⁄₁₆"-dia. guide hole (for the lag screw that secures the shaft to the tower) through the top edge of the shaft, 9" from the front end. Also drill a ¼"-dia. pilot hole in the center of the front end of the shaft.

MAKE THE BLADES & HUB. Cut the propeller blades (L)

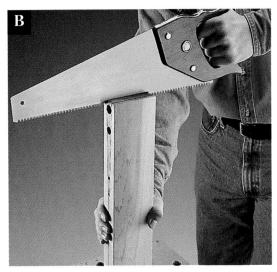

Drill holes of varying diameter to create an outline, then cut a slot for the tail into the shaft.

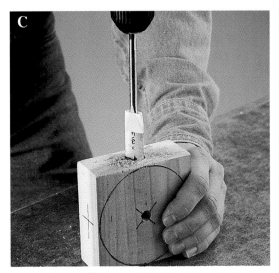

Drill ¾"-dia. × 1"-deep guide holes into the four sides of the hub to hold the backer rods.

and hub (M) to the full sizes listed in the *Cutting List*. On the thin edge of each blade board, draw a cutting line so the blade tapers from 7" in width at one end to 2" in width at the other end. Cut the blades to shape with a circular saw. To make the circular hub, first draw diagonal lines between opposite corners on the face of the hub board. Set the point of a compass at the intersection point of the diagonal lines, and draw a circle with a 2" radius. Drill a ⅞"-dia. hole through the centerpoint. Then mark drilling points on all four edges of the hub board, centered end to end and side to side, for drilling the holes that will hold the backer rods. Install a ¾"-dia. spade bit in your drill, then wrap a piece of masking tape 1" up from the bottom of the cutting part of the bit. Use the masking tape as a guide for stopping the holes when they reach 1" in depth. Drill ¾"-dia. × 1"-deep holes at the centerpoints in each edge of the hub board **(photo C).** Cut out the hub with a jig saw, following the round cutting line. Cut the

backer rods (N) from ¾" doweling, then sand a flat edge onto each rod, using a belt sander. Stop the flat edges 1" from the end of each dowel (this creates a flat mounting surface).

ASSEMBLE THE PROPELLER. Attach the thick edge of each blade to the flat surface of a backer rod with three #4 × 1" panhead screws and epoxy glue **(photo D).** Apply epoxy glue to the tail where it meets the shaft, and fasten it in the slot with 1¼" deck screws. Before proceeding, apply exterior wood stain to all the wood parts, and apply paste wax in the guide holes in the hub and shaft. Attach the blade assembly to the shaft with a ⅜ × 6" lag screw and pairs of 1"-dia. nylon washers inserted on each side of the hub. Fasten the shaft to the tower with a ⅜ × 6" lag screw and pairs of nylon

washers at the top and bottom edges of the shaft. Do not overtighten the screws.

SET UP THE WINDMILL. Position the 4 × 4 frame in the desired location in your yard or garden. Cut the stakes (O), sharpening one end of each stake. Attach the stakes at the inside corners of the foot frame with screws, then drive the stakes into the ground. Attach the base frame to the foot frame with counterbored lag screws. Drive counterbored lag screws through the base sides and into the foot ends.

Glue the ends of the backer rods into the holes in the hub to mount the propeller blades.

Doghouse

Add a contemporary twist to a traditional backyard project with this cedar-trimmed, arched-entry doghouse.

CONSTRUCTION MATERIALS

Quantity	Lumber
2	1 × 2" × 8' cedar
3	2 × 2" × 8' pine
2	2 × 4" × 8' cedar
1	⅝" × 4 × 8' siding
1	¾" × 4 × 8' ABX plywood

Close your eyes and picture the first image that comes to mind when you think of a doghouse. More than likely it's a boxy, boring little structure. Now consider this updated doghouse, with its sheltered breezeway and contemporary styling. What dog wouldn't want to call this distinctive dwelling home? The

sturdy 2 × 4 frame provides a stable foundation for the wall panels and roof. The main area has plenty of room to house an average-size dog comfortably, and the porch area shelters the entry, while providing an open, shady area for your pet to relax. The rounded feet keep the inside of the house dry by raising the base up off the ground.

OVERALL SIZE:
30" HIGH
27¼" WIDE
48" LONG

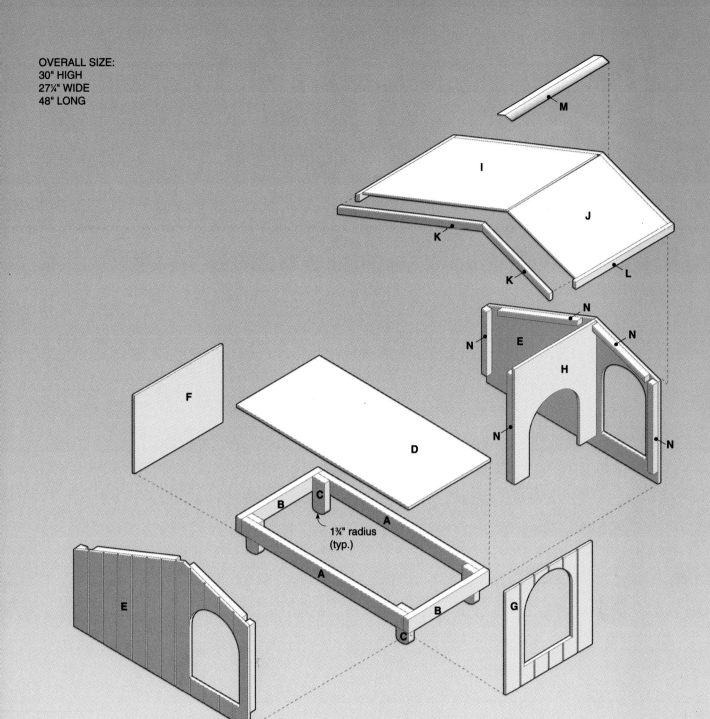

1¾" radius (typ.)

Key	Part	Dimension	Pcs.	Material
	Cutting List			
A	Frame side	1½ × 3½ × 45"	2	Cedar
B	Frame end	1½ × 3½ × 22⅞"	2	Cedar
C	Feet	1½ × 3½ × 7½"	4	Cedar
D	Floor	¾ × 22⅞ × 48"	1	ABX Plywood
E	Side panel	⅝ × 30 × 48"	2	Siding
F	House end panel	⅝ × 18 × 24"	1	Siding
G	Porch end panel	⅝ × 24 × 24"	1	Siding

Key	Part	Dimension	Pcs.	Material
	Cutting List			
H	Center panel	⅝ × 22⅞ × 29¾"	1	Siding
I	House roof	¾ × 25½ × 35"	1	ABX Plywood
J	Porch roof	¾ × 25½ × 23"	1	ABX Plywood
K	Side roof trim	⅞ × 1½ × *"	4	Cedar
L	End roof trim	⅞ × 1½ × 27¼"	2	Cedar
M	Flashing	1⁄16 × 4 × 27¼"	1	Galv. flashing
N	Cleat	1½ × 1½ × *"	10	Pine

Materials: Deck screws (2", 3"), 6d galvanized finish nails, 2d galvanized common nails, silicone caulk, roofing nails with rubber washers, finishing materials.

*****Cut to fit**   **Note:** Measurements reflect the actual size of dimensional lumber.

Fasten the 2 × 4 cedar feet to the inside frame corners with 3" galvanized deck screws.

Lay out the roof angle on the side panels using a straightedge.

Directions: Doghouse

BUILD THE FRAME & FLOOR. The frame of the doghouse is the foundation for the floor, sides and roof. It is simply built from 2 × 4 cedar lumber. Start by cutting the frame sides (A) and frame ends (B) to length. Place the frame sides between the frame ends to form a rectangle, then fasten together with 3" deck screws. Make sure to keep the outside edges flush. Next, cut the feet (C) to length. Use a compass to lay out a 1¾"-radius roundover curve on one end of each foot, then cut with a jig saw to form the roundover. Smooth out the jig-saw cuts with a power sander. Fasten a foot in each corner of the frame with 3" deck screws **(photo A)**. Be sure to keep the top edges of the feet flush with the top edges of the frame. After the frame has been assembled, cut the floor (D) to size from ¾"-thick exterior plywood and fasten it to the top of the frame with 2" deck screws. The edges of the floor should be flush with the outside edges of the frame.

MAKE THE WALLS. The walls for the doghouse are cut from ⅝"-thick siding panels—we chose panels with grooves cut every 4" for a more decorative effect. Start by cutting the side panels (E) to the full size listed in the *Cutting List* on page 93. Then, make angled cuts that form a peak on the top of the panel to create the roof line. To make the cuts, first mark points 18" up from the bottom on one end, and 24" up from the bot-

> **TIP**
>
> *With most siding products, whether they are sheet goods or lap siding boards, there is a definite front and back face. In some cases, it is very easy to tell which face is meant to be exposed, but you always need to be careful not to confuse the two.*

tom on the other end. Then, measure in along the top edge 30" out from the end with the 24" mark, and mark a point to indicate the peak of the roof. Connect the peak mark to the marks on the ends with straight

lines to create the cutting lines **(photo B).** Lay the side panels on top of one another, fastening them with a screw or two in the waste area. Then cut both panels at the same time, using a circular saw or jig saw and straightedge cutting guide. To make the arched cutouts in the front (taller) sections of the side panels, first measure and mark points 2" and 16" in from the 24"-tall end of one panel, then draw lines from the bottom to the top of the panel, through the points. Measure up 4¼" and 15¾" from the bottom edge and draw horizontal lines to complete the square. Find the centerpoint between the sides of the square cutout outline, and measure down 7" from the top of the cutout at that point. Press down on the end of a ruler so it pivots at that point, and use the ruler and a pencil like a compass to draw a curve with a 7" radius across the top of the cutout **(photo C).** Drill a starter hole at a corner of the cutout outline, then cut the opening with a jig saw **(photo D).** Trace the cutout onto the other side panel, then make that

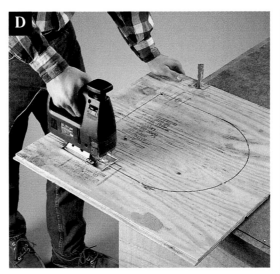

Lay out the opening archway on the side panels using a ruler and pencil.

Cut out the openings in the panels with a jig saw.

cutout. One of the side panels can also be used as a template for marking the arched cutout in the center panel and the porch end panel. First, cut the center panel (H) and porch end panel (G) to full size. Trace an arched cutout outline onto the porch end panel so the sides are 4½" from each side edge and the top is 15¾" up from the bottom. Mark an arched cutout outline on the center panel, 3⅞" from each

side edge and 15¾" up from the bottom. Make the cutouts with a jig saw, then sand all cut edges smooth.

ATTACH THE WALLS & FRAME. Cut the house end panel (F). Fasten the side panels to the frame with 2" deck screws, so the bottoms of the panels are flush with the bottoms of the frame, and the ends of the panels are flush with the frame ends. Fasten the house end panel and the porch end panel

to the frame so the bottoms of the panels are flush with the bottom of the frame (the sides of the end panels will overlap the side panels by ⅝" on each side). The 10 cleats (N) in the doghouse are used to create attaching surfaces for the roof panels and the center panel, and to tie the panel walls together. Cut them long enough to fit in the positions shown in the *Diagram* on page 93—there should be a little space between the ends of the cleats, so exact cutting is not important. Just make sure the edges are flush with the edges of the panel they are attached to. Cut the 10 cleats (N) from 2 × 2 pine, and fasten four cleats along the perimeter of each side panel, using 2" deck screws. Fasten the remaining two cleats at the edges of the back side of the center panel. Then, set the center panel between the side panels so the

TIP

If plan dimensions do not meet your needs, you can recalculate them to a different scale. The doghouse shown here is designed for an average dog (about 15" tall). If you own a larger dog, add 1" to the size of the entry cutouts and panels for every inch that your dog is taller than 15".

Fasten the center panel by driving screws through the side panels into the cleats. Use a combination square to keep the panel even.

Cut each side roof trim piece to fit between the peak and the end of the roof panel, mitering the ends so they will be perpendicular when installed. Attach all the roof trim pieces with galvanized finish nails.

backsaw. Attach the trim pieces to the side panels with 6d galvanized finish nails **(photo F).**

APPLY FINISHING TOUCHES. Sand all the wood surfaces smooth, paying special attention to any sharp edges, then prime and paint the doghouse. Use a good-quality exterior primer and at least two coats of paint, or you can do as we did and simply apply two or three coats of nontoxic sealant to preserve the natural wood tones. We used linseed oil. When the finish has dried thoroughly, cut a strip of galvanized steel flashing (M) to cover the roof peak (or you can use aluminum flashing if you prefer). Use tin snips or aviator snips to cut the flashing, and buff the edges with emery paper to help smooth out any sharp points. Lay the flashing lengthwise on a wood scrap, so the flashing overhangs by 2". Bend the flashing over the edge of the board to create a nice, crisp peak, then attach the flashing with roofing nails with neoprene (rubber) washers driven at 4" intervals **(photo G).**

front is aligned with the peak in the roof. Make sure the center panel is perpendicular, and attach it with 2" deck screws driven through the side panels and into the cleats at the edges of the center panel **(photo E).**

ATTACH THE ROOF & TRIM. The roof and trim are the final structural elements to be fastened to the doghouse. Cut the house roof (I) and porch roof (J) to size from ¾"-thick exterior plywood. Fasten the roof panels to the cleats at the tops of the side walls, making sure the edges of the panels butt together to form the roof peak. Next, cut the trim pieces to frame the roof (K, L) from 1 × 2 cedar. The end roof trim pieces are square-cut at the ends, but the ends of the side roof trim pieces (K) need to be miter-cut to form clean joints at the peak and at the ends, where they

will meet the end trim. To mark the side trim pieces for cutting, first cut the side trim pieces so they are an inch or two longer than the space between the end of the roof panel and the roof peak. Lay each rough trim piece in position, flush with the top of the roof panel. On each trim piece, mark a vertical cutoff line that is aligned with the end of the roof panel. Then, mark a cutoff line at the peak, making sure the line is perpendicular to the peak. Cut the trim pieces with a power miter saw or miter box and

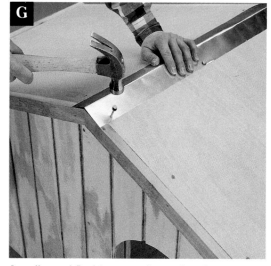

Install metal flashing over the roof peak, using roofing nails with rubber washers.